No Instant Grapes in God's Vineyard

DISCIPLINES for SPIRITUAL GROWTH

Louise C. Spiker

Judson Press® Valley Forge

Unless otherwise indicated, Bible quotations in this volume are from Today's English Version, the *Good News Bible*—Old Testament: Copyright © American Bible Society, 1976; New Testament: Copyright © American Bible Society 1966, 1971, 1976. Used by permission.
Other versions of the Bible quoted in this book are:
The New English Bible, Copyright © The Delegates of the Oxford University Press and The Syndics of the Cambridge University Press, 1961, 1970.
The New Testament in Modern English, Rev. Ed. Copyright © J. B. Phillips 1972. Used by permission of The Macmillan Company and Geoffrey Bles, Ltd.
The Revised Standard Version of the Bible copyrighted 1946, 1952 © 1971, 1973 by the Division of Christian Education of the National Council of the Churches of Christ in the U.S.A., and used by permission.
The Jerusalem Bible, copyright © 1966 by Darton, Longman & Todd, Ltd. and Doubleday and Company, Inc. Used by permission of the publisher.
The Cotton Patch Version of Luke & Acts by Clarence Jordan © 1969. By permission of New Century Publishers, Inc., Piscataway, New Jersey 08854.

Library of Congress Cataloging in Publication Data

Spiker, Louise C.
  No instant grapes in God's vineyard.

  Includes bibliographical references.
  1. Spiritual life.   I. Title.
BV4501.2.S7135   1982   248.4   82-13993
ISBN 0-8170-0955-8

The name JUDSON PRESS is registered as a trademark in the U.S. Patent Office.
Printed in the U.S.A. ⊕

to the Seekers,
my special Love group,
and to all seekers of the Truth

Contents

Preface

I am an ordinary woman loved by an extraordinary God. While the accident of my birth placed me in the mainstream Christian tradition via home, church, and country, the fullness of this love did not reach me until I became intentional about keeping Christian disciplines. The notion that discipline is liberating was a new one to me, but the evident joy and power in mission group members of the Church of the Saviour, Washington, D.C., enticed me to try keeping spiritual disciplines. Instead of talking only to God and trying to be good, I began listening to God and asking for guidance. It has proved to be harder and more painful than I expected, but also richer and better than I had dared hope. For me, there is no other way. I simply don't know how to live my outer life—relating to persons—without the inner one—relating to God personally in a daily quiet time.

I never intended to be a writer. But then Moses did not plan to be a speaker, especially before a king; Amos did not start out as a prophet; Saul persecuted Christians before he believed in Jesus Christ. Changes, conversions, new directions are what the Creator is always about! I will admit I am addicted to words and the meaning they convey and the possibilities they hold for communication with persons I may never meet. I have lived long enough to realize both the uniqueness and the relatedness of my life journey to other Christian pilgrims. So many authors have fostered my spiritual growth by their writings that I dare to hope my sharing may help others.

I have risked sharing my inner life in the hope that I may encourage readers to be similarly honest and open with God; depth relationships, with either humans or the Divine, require intimacy. I tell of some of the quiet places and times other disciples and I have found to be refreshing, healing, and growth producing. Jesus always invites his followers, "'Come with me, by yourselves, to some lonely place where you can rest quietly.' (For they had no leisure even to eat, so many were coming and going)" (Mark 6:31, NEB). This book is about those quiet places. It tells of things we can do to put ourselves in the most likely spots to let in God's love and grace. God wants to bless and empower us. Let us prepare to receive.

This book is suitable for personal use and/or in small groups. If you are a member of a church board, committee, task force, or a study or prayer group, you may wish to invite the other members to explore these practices with you. Groups who share together in prayer and Bible study will almost certainly work together more effectively in mission. If you are just beginning to keep spiritual disciplines, using this book in a small group is highly desirable. You may wish to start one. I have initiated several groups when I wanted fellow pilgrims and experimenters. How? I invited people to my house. I made announcements in church. I put an invitation in the church newsletter, and I spoke with friends individually. Often I felt like "a voice crying in the wilderness," but each time someone responded. I made lots of mistakes, and so these groups were good learning experiences. (Elizabeth O'Connor says we learn more from our mistakes than from our successes.) The human sharing and caring experienced in such a group feels so good. Best of all, Jesus keeps his promise, "For where two or three come together in my name, I am there with them" (Matthew 18:20, TEV).

Long lists are forbidding to me, so I have not compiled a bibliography. I suggest using the notes at the bottom of the pages as sources for further reading. Almost all the books I have quoted from are in my personal library and are much used and underlined. Still, there is no way I can know what is meaningful to you. There are many resources available. So much depends on the right book, experience, conversation, workshop, at the right time. My best advice is to pray and be open to the leading of the Holy Spirit. God has a very personal interest in your spiritual growth. Seek, and let God provide.

It is important to me to thank the Wellspring mission group of the Church of the Saviour, Washington, D.C. Without them I would not be the person who wrote this book. Even more so, without Judith Roark as spiritual friend and guide to channel God's love most personally to me, I would have lost my way on the inward, outward journey. My gratitude also to my friend Vergie Gillespie, who knew I was a writer before I did. Thanks also to my husband, Ralph, and two special friends, Betty Gale and Joy Lyness, for their indispensable support in most practical ways.

Introduction:
Spiritual Growth—What Is It?

"The little child grew up and became strong in spirit" (Luke 1:80a, Phillips). We, too, are called to grow and keep growing. To nurture our spiritual growth we must *be intentional about taking time to develop an inner awareness of our relationship to God and all God's creation.* Spiritual growth is not separate, unrelated, otherworldly, pietistic. We need to recognize the reality of both the material *and* the spiritual, the conscious *and* the unconscious, and their interrelatedness. It is not a matter of either/or, but of both/and. The goal of Christian spirituality is connectedness with our everyday world, God's world, the only world we've got.

Jesus ate, drank, partied, healed, helped, related. *But* to do all this effectively he had to withdraw periodically and often, for time alone with himself and God—to look deeply within himself to discover the uniqueness and purpose of his life and to be in touch with the Father for guidance and power.

The resurrected Christ told his eleven faithful disciples, "But you must wait in the city until the power from above comes down upon you" (Luke 24:49b, TEV). We must wait, for the Holy Spirit comes not on demand, but as gift. The Quaker author Richard J. Foster speaks of "the way of disciplined grace."

> It is "grace" because it is free; it is "disciplined" because there is something for us to do. In *The Cost of Discipleship* Dietrich Bonhoeffer made clear that grace is free, but it is not cheap. Once we clearly understand that God's grace is unearned and unearnable, and if we expect to grow, we must take up a consciously chosen course of action involving both individual and group life. That is the purpose of the Spiritual Disciplines.[1]

Tho Truth is so marvelous and awe-ful, and listeners (readers) so varied in temperament and life stages that I want to use any

[1] Richard J. Foster, *Celebration of Discipline* (New York: Harper & Row, Publishers, Inc., 1978), pp. 6, 7.

and all possibilities to reach persons wherever they are. Jesus often used parables to convey his message. Following are some metaphors to which I am particularly addicted and that will undoubtedly keep popping up in the following pages. I hope one or more will have special meaning for you or will lead you to your own. Morton Kelsey points out that "The important thing is to work with one's own images that come in meditation, relating them to the great symbols of our religion."[2] My favorites are:

- *Growth, seeds, gardening.* A poem fragment that was on my mother's dresser when I was growing up says, ". . . One is nearer God's heart in a garden than anywhere else on earth." God is more than nature, but nature is because God created.
- *Connectedness.* Branches being connected to the Vine is the theme of the first chapter. Symbiotic relationships in nature and between persons abound, and they all delight and comfort me.
- *Inner, outer journey.* Life is a journey and it has become evident to me that I need the inner, quiet journey to my Center to sustain and give direction to my work in the outer world.
- *Digesting the holy.* Digestion is a God-given process of our bodies, partly voluntary (biting, chewing, swallowing) and partly involuntary (stomach enzymes and the intestinal process) which is analogous to the intentional part of the spiritual growth which needs our action and the grace part which is given by God. As we take more of God into ourselves and digest (integrate) Truth in our everyday lives, we become more truly part of the body of Christ.
- *A ministry and a sabbath.* "There is something very deep in our tradition, a kind of foundational spiritual discipline of the Christian way, as well as the Jewish way, where there is a clear sense that we are meant to move between two 'in touch' qualities of time: Ministry and Sabbath, united by a single-hearted awareness of the Spirit through all times."[3]

Spiritual growth is growing toward wholeness or holiness, which are closely related. Wholeness implies a completeness, a recognition of our dark side as well as our light. Dealing with our sins as well as our virtues is humbling and produces an understanding and closeness to other sinners. Spirituality is definitely not otherworldly, holier-than-thou attitudes. If you are not becoming more appealing to your spouse, friend, children, parents, co-work-

[2]Morton T. Kelsey, *The Other Side of Silence* (New York: Paulist Press, 1976), p. 208.

[3]Tilden Edwards, "Keeping the Sabbath," *Alban Institute Action Information* (November-December, 1981), p. 1.

ers, you are not growing spiritually. As Paul writes, "But the Spirit produces love, joy, peace, patience, kindness, goodness, faithfulness, humility, and self-control" (Galatians 5:22, TEV). If others see these traits flowing from you, from the inside out, you are growing spiritually.

1

Remain in the Vine

Suppose someone convinced you that Jesus was speaking to-morrow in the next town. Would you take a day of vacation from work and go? Would you postpone the shopping or laundry and arrange to get the car and go? Would you stay up late or get up early to get something essential done so that you could go and still meet your obligations?

What if Jesus were the featured speaker at a weekend conference one hundred to five hundred miles away? Would you cut corners on the food budget, drink water at coffee break, forego a new tennis racket, not send the children to camp, even borrow money, so the whole family could attend?

"Yes—yes, of course!" you (and I) answer immediately. It would be fantastic! The chance of a lifetime! Seeing, hearing, touching Jesus would change my life. I know his love, his power, his au-thority in speaking of the Eternal would reach me and motivate me in a way that eludes me now. Experience—that's what I need, real life experience. Reading is good sometimes. I can think of a few books that have moved me—for a time. Films and TV some-times give me new insights into Bible times and shed light on a parable or saying of Jesus, although anyone actually portraying Jesus makes me uncomfortable. But a firsthand experience with Jesus—*that* would make a difference. Experiencing is how I learn. It is what makes it possible for me to change. Yes! Experience with Jesus. That's what I want!

If we really want it, we can have it. Not with the historical Jesus. He was crucified. But with the risen Christ. God resurrected him. Jesus Christ is available to all. It's not a new idea. I didn't make it up. The apostles knew it, although they were slow learners like I am. Paul met the risen Christ most unexpectedly, which caused him to make a sudden change in his life direction. St. Augustine and many others experienced God so personally and lived so differently because of their intimacy with God, that the rest of us call them saints. And countless others through the ages and still today, in less publicized but just as significant ways, meet the risen Christ and live out his will in their daily lives. As Paul told the Romans, "Don't let the world around you squeeze you into its own mold, but let God remold your minds from within, so that you may prove in practice that the plan of God for you is good, meets all his demands and moves toward the goal of true maturity" (Romans 12:2, Phillips).

WHY SO HARD?

Yes, it's possible. It has been and is being done. There are models to follow. God's presence in individual lives has been and continues to be written about and put into print (such as in this book, for instance). I am referring to a spiritual experience: an attentiveness to the inner life, to the reality of God within you, loving and guiding you. But such an experience is not common in today's world, even in the church. Most Christians do not regularly practice the time-honored Christian disciplines—spending time daily in prayer, meditation, keeping a journal, Bible study, or similar quiet moments. Why? Why would we abandon our well-laid plans and rush off to see the historical Jesus if we fail to find time to meet the risen Christ? While I can't answer for you, I do want to suggest some reasons that influence me.

First, we live in a rational, materialistic culture based on science and technology, a culture that at best laughs at or ignores the spiritual world and at worst denies it. If something cannot be recognized by one of our five senses or measured and tested by their extensions (scientific instruments), by current standards it doesn't exist. Our Western world is so exclusively identified with the external physical world that persons who want to investigate the inner spiritual world often turn to Eastern religions and transcendental meditation for help, apparently oblivious to the Christian tradition of meditation. Not many persons believe and act on the fact that in addition to the visible "outer" space-time world there is also an invisible, inner, just as real, spiritual world.

A very different world view existed when the Bible was written, one that assumed the reality of both the physical and spiritual realms, including demonic and angelic powers. Jesus talked about both in his frequent parables: illustrations from the physical world pointed to truths in the spiritual world.

Second, our comfortable life-styles—the good life as portrayed by our multitudinous advertisements—demand that we spend much time, money, and energy making a living. We are busy, very busy, taking care of our families' needs, doing some good deeds, keeping informed about the world, meeting obligations that seem reasonable when looked at one at a time, but somehow add up to more than we can comfortably handle. How can we possibly find time for one more thing, even a very good thing, in our action-packed lives? Time often seems like our most precious commodity.

Third, most of us don't realize that:

> There are two churches: the Church, the institution, and the Church, the People of God. In the Church, the institution, there are two orders, clergy and lay. In the Church, the People of God, there are varieties of gifts and functions. *The two are NOT identical.* The institution is the earthen vessel in which the treasure is kept. It is NOT the treasure. . . . The institutional Church is very necessary, has always been necessary, in time will always be necessary. Without it the Church, the People of God, would not exist. The institutional Church is God's instrument for preserving God's people.[1]

When we are aware of *only* the institutional church, we function within a system like any other institution. We tend to rely on the wisdom of those in authority and on established decision-making procedures, and often neglect to develop our own direct communication with God. Most churches provide more opportunities and encouragement to their members to serve on boards and committees in the local church than to become the people of God, on mission in the world. The inner journey, the encounter with the risen Christ, is not essential to maintain the institutional church.

Fourth, meeting the risen Christ is a grace experience. We can't earn it. God gives because God is a giver. As Paul says, "But if it is by grace, then it does not rest on deeds done, or grace would cease to be grace" (Romans 11:6, NEB). God's way is the opposite of the "You can't get something for nothing" philosophy generally operative in our society. We are used to earning our way, being rewarded when we deserve it. "But God has shown us how much he loves us—it was while we were still sinners that Christ died for us!" (Romans 5:8, TEV). Not payment or reward, but a gift! It goes against our grain, perhaps even our "religion," to sit down and learn how to "be" rather than to "do." But waiting is the proper preparation for meeting the risen Christ. Grace is so uncommon in our everyday world that the song calls it "Amazing Grace."

While these reasons are not exhaustive, they indicate the variety and strength of the opposition surrounding us. In our society it is incredibly difficult to make and keep a commitment to daily time for Christian disciplines so that we may grow spiritually. While the United States usually proclaims itself a Christian nation, being a committed Christian and living by Jesus' teachings is as much a counterculture activity today as it was when Caesar

---

[1] Verna J. Dozier, "Toward a Theology of the Laity," *Alban Institute Action Information* (September, 1979).

reigned. Believing—and acting on that belief—that God is know-able, meetable, present personally, is neither popular nor easy.

BUT HOW CAN I DO WITHOUT?

If keeping Christian disciplines is incredibly difficult, trying to live a Christian servant-person life-style without them, without the felt presence of God personally, is infinitely harder, if not impossible. How can we know what we are to be about as unique creatures in God's creation, if we aren't in touch with God daily? If we only know *about* the resurrection but do not feel Christ rising *in us,* we are impoverished onlookers, at the fringes of the crowd, who gather to see and hear Jesus. We need time alone with Christ to be graced by his presence, empowered by his spirit.

In John's Gospel, chapters fourteen through seventeen, the familiar "I am" passages give a clear picture of the relationship Jesus has with his Parent and desires to have with faithful disciples (learners). Judas has just left. Before that Jesus acted out his servant-leadership style by washing his disciples' feet. Ahead is denial and crucifixion. This is certainly no time for small talk. No, these words are the summation of all that Jesus wants his committed followers to know.

The author (tradition says it is John, the son of Zebedee, the beloved disciple) both walked with Jesus in Galilee and saw the risen Christ. His "good news" was most likely written toward the end of the first century as the Christian community realized that the generation who knew the historical Jesus personally was dying. The point is that these words are the result of the individual and/or collective memory of those who knew both the historical Jesus and the risen Christ, through the Holy Spirit.

A first reaction to any report written seventy years after the event might be to conclude that it could not be very accurate. If we consider only the "six o'clock evening news" perspective, that is a logical conclusion. The former fisherman, however, is sharing his remembrance and understanding of Jesus' message after the passage of these years, illuminated by the guidance of the Holy Spirit. John can now tell not only what Jesus said, but also what Jesus meant. It has a *"Now* I know what he was talking about" sureness. This full comprehension matches his remembrance of what Jesus promised, "I have said all this while I am still with you. But the one who is coming to stand by you, the Holy Spirit whom the Father will send in my name, will be your teacher and will bring to your minds all that I have said to you" (John 14:25, 36, Phillips). Sometimes we tell our children, "You'll understand that when you are older." The same is true of all of us, then and now. Not that time automatically adds wisdom, but it does give opportunity for reflection on the meaning of our experiences. If we allow the risen Christ to be a part of our reflection, we are open to Truth, not just facts.

So, to those of us who would change plans to see the historical Jesus, but have trouble finding the time or the route to meet the risen Christ, what does the writer of John, who has known both, have to say?

REMAIN IN THE VINE

We had grape arbors in our yard when I was growing up. My father grew grapevines from a single cutting. He planted, fertilized, cultivated, pruned, waited, and enjoyed the fruit. For over half the year the vines were dead-looking—brown, gnarled, twisted trunks—sturdy and interestingly shaped, rooted firmly in the earth, but apparently lifeless. Each spring green shoots appeared, then vines and leaves grew in profusion until all the brown was covered and even the support arbor was hidden in the abundance of green growth. In summer, green grapes appeared and in September we ate the purple grapes. My mother made jelly and grape juice for winter use out of the wild varieties called "fox grapes."

It is this image I see, this I think of, when I read John 15. All kinds of parables, glimpses of truth, connections reach out to me, like the appealing curled tendrils of the vines.

"I am the real vine, and my Father is the gardener" (John 15:1, TEV). God is the Creator and Sustainer of life—all life, including my life. God is God. I may not like or understand God's timing or ways, but God provides all that is necessary for life and growth—sunshine and rain, fertilizer and pruning, soil for roots, and sky for reaching toward.

Jesus, the Vine, was so long dormant. He had an active recorded ministry of only three years after thirty years of preparation and/or waiting. To a culture like ours which values "doing" over "being," it doesn't make much sense. Yet for almost 2,000 years Christian "branches" have continued to shoot out from that Vine and to bear abundant fruit. From the Gospels it is clear that during his active ministry there was a rhythm of times of ministering and times of quiet retreat to be with the Father.

"He breaks off every branch in me that does not bear fruit, and he prunes every branch that does bear fruit, so that it will be clean and bear more fruit" (John 15:2, TEV). Pruning produces a better yield, but it takes a certain courage to cut off perfectly healthy parts of a growing plant. I remember Daddy pruned severely because it was the way to get more grapes. Jesus went on to tell his disciples, "You have been made clean already by the teaching I have given you" (John 15:3, TEV). I am not sure that many of us today are full enough of Jesus' teaching to be considered "clean already." Perhaps we need to do some pruning of our lives.

Pruning is a cutting off, a ridding ourselves of something. There are only twenty-four hours in a day. To make time to absorb more of Jesus' teaching, we may have to cut out something we are now doing.

Each midsummer when the bunches of green grapes had formed, my parents spent several evenings slipping paper bags over each bunch and securing them with pins. This destroyed the completely natural beauty of the vine, so there had to be an important reason. There was. It kept the bees from stinging and thus spoiling the grapes. This reminds me of the warning Jesus gave, "If the world hates you, just remember that it has hated me first" (John 15:18, TEV). We need protection if we attempt the counterculture Jesus way, and it is available: the Comforter, the Spirit. Not a visible wrapping, but an invisible, powerful protection for those who stay closely connected to the Vine.

NO INSTANT GRAPES

To "bear much fruit"—how appealing! Why, even the world rewards those who produce notable results: Nobel prizes for Martin Luther King, Jr., and Mother Teresa. But when? Years and years after they began growing. After years and years of remaining in the Vine. The power and patience to produce that kind of fruit is rare indeed. Many (most?) of us feel powerless to make a significant difference about the many situations that offend us and God— poverty, racism, the armaments race, environmental abuse—yet Jesus' words are clear, "If you remain in me and my words remain in you, then you will ask for anything you wish, and you shall have it" (John 15:7, TEV). The promise and the power are available. To "bear much fruit" we need only be shoots connected to the Vine, to experience the risen Christ.

The significance of the vine imagery used by Jesus was known to the original listeners. From the bunches of grapes so heavy that two men were needed to carry them back from the Promised Land to the waiting Israelites, to Isaiah's song of the vineyard that yielded sour grapes, the Hebrews knew they were God's special vineyard. They were the few, the Chosen People of God. Then Jesus says that he is the Chosen One, and uses the fruit of the vine to symbolize the shedding of his blood for all people. The vine is associated with the calling out of the few. So it still is today. Those who prune their lives to keep Christian disciplines and are willing to be pruned by the Vine-dresser are the minority. Jesus was not talking to the crowds in John 15, but to his disciples, the dedicated few who had walked with him for three years.

Jesus invites us today to come out from the crowd, to walk close to him, as close as a vine shoot is to the vine trunk. But to be today's Chosen People, to be a Chosen Person, *we must choose to* be connected to the Vine. One of my many selves[2] responds eagerly, positively. But there is also a self that knows I don't always follow through on my good intentions. Another self is afraid of the cost: Will I have to give up my comfortable life-style? Will I be considered too different, a "kook," by my friends? Another self considers it just downright unrealistic, considering my daily schedule and responsibilities. How? How can I be a more faithful follower? How can I keep Christian disciplines? Isn't that for sinners? How? How? How?

Relax. One of the most comforting Bible verses I know, ranking right up there with, "The Lord is my shepherd; I shall want nothing" (Psalm 23:1, NEB) is, "Thus Abram journeyed by stages toward . . ." (Genesis 12:9, NEB). We don't have to arrive today— or even tomorrow. God doesn't expect us suddenly to be spiritual giants or magnificent achievers. No, God called forth Abram (later called Abraham) to be who he was created to be. God wants to lead us to our real selves, step by step, stage by stage. Even when we backslide, as Abram did while detouring in Egypt when he opted for self-security by passing off Sarah, his wife, as his sister, God was/is patient, forgiving, and steadfast.

The grapevine and the entire plant world are visual reminders of the slow gradual growth process, the divine structure, that produces fruit in its season. With a purple crayon you can quickly draw a recognizable grape cluster. With a few dollars you can easily purchase a decorative wax or sparkling glass bunch of grapes. But a real, sweet, juicy, luscious handful of grapes takes a long, long time from seed to fruit. God instituted that process. The Gardener understands that you need growing time before you bloom and bear fruit.

Growth requires not only time but also nurturing, some specific acts of care. "Nurturing Silence in a Noisy Heart"[3] does not happen without intentionality. Nurturing ourselves, taking care of ourselves, *is not selfish.* When we abbreviate Jesus' second commandment to "love others" forgetting "as yourself," we distort it. Worse, we negate it because it is not possible to love others if we do not love ourselves. If we wish to grow spiritually, we must nourish ourselves with spiritual food and drink and grace ourselves with quiet resting times. We do not live by bread alone.

[2] Elizabeth O'Connor has written an excellent book, *Our Many Selves, A Handbook for Self-Discovery* (New York: Harper & Row, Publishers, Inc., 1971).

[3] Wayne E. Oates's book *Nurturing Silence in a Noisy Heart* (Garden City, New York: Doubleday & Co., Inc., 1979) gives many specific helps for finding quiet in our contemporary life-style.

ANY PRECEDENTS?

What have God's people done and what do they do to nurture their spiritual growth? Bible reading is basic. The psalmist sings:

> the law of the LORD is his delight,
> the law his meditation night and day.
>   He is like a tree
> planted beside a watercourse,
> which yields its fruit in season
>   and its leaf never withers. . . .
>   —Psalm 1:2-3, NEB

Likewise, the many references to Old Testament laws, history, and persons by Jesus, Paul, Stephen, and others confirm their familiarity with our basic text. The Living Word feeds those who read and study it.

A time and place apart is valued in countless lives through the ages. Two significant events of Jacob's life—his ladder dream and wrestling match—happened when he was alone in open country. Moses and the Israelites spent forty years in the wilderness learning how to be a community. David composed psalms during his solitary sheepherding days. Amos, another shepherd, heard God's call to prophesy while in the semidesert hills near Tekoa. Jesus crossed the lake, retreated to a garden, went to the wilderness to restore his soul in God's presence. Slow travel methods left Paul with large blocks of time to reflect and meditate between visiting young churches. Paul, John the Divine (author of Revelation), early missionaries such as Adoniram Judson, and more recently Martin Luther King, Jr., have even used the solitariness of prison for prayer, writing, and growth. A centuries-old Russian custom involves going to a *poustinia,* a barren hut away from all, to be led by the Lord into the desert of one's own (the *poustinik's*) heart— there to learn how to serve God better. Monasteries have been part of Christianity since A.D. 200. Roman Catholics have a long tradition of "making a retreat." Friends (Quakers) meet silently for worship.

Corporate worship is a public acknowledgement of our dependence on God and time taken to praise and be with God. "I was glad when they said to me, 'Let us go to the LORD'S house'" (Psalm 122:1, TEV). Jesus went to the synagogue "as his custom was." From the simple rock-stacked altars of Abram to the wide variety of architecture and worship forms of today, regular worship has always been a central discipline and joy for God's faithful people.

As children of God, followers of Jesus, we need to be in touch with our Leader. Prayer is communication with God—listening and speaking. If Jesus needed prayer, as is recorded in Scripture, how much more do we!

Keeping a journal can be a form of prayer, confession, reflection, and/or self-knowledge, but is most importantly a place for being honest with oneself and with God. St. Augustine, John Woolman, and George Fox, along with an increasing number of modern Christians, were journal writers.

Dreams were crucial in the careers of the Old Testament Joseph and Jesus' earthly father, plus many other Bible persons. John Sanford calls dreams "God's forgotten language."[4] Scientists are certain we all dream every night. Dreams originate in our depths. An openness to them and a willingness to write them down and ponder them can open a window to God.

Money—earning, giving, and spending it—is mentioned frequently in the Bible. The many facets of this vital subject are evident in the various biblical references: the Old Testament tithing law, Jesus praising the widow's mite, the Sermon on the Mount, the parable of the talents, the parable of all workers who were paid the same, Paul's advice on cheerful giving—to name a few. We need to pray much and ponder deeply to deal responsibly with our life-styles, earning power, possessions, and giving. Since this important discipline is not dealt with in this book, I encourage you to read Richard J. Foster's *Freedom of Simplicity*.[5] He takes a thorough look at this complex subject from the Old Testament teaching to the world you and I live in today.

The Jewish and Christian tradition of fasting is abstaining from food for spiritual purposes. This is distinctly different from dieting for health or vanity reasons. Moses, David, Elijah, Esther, Daniel, Anna, Paul, and, of course, Jesus, fasted. Fasting frees us from what normally controls us, so that we may better focus on God.

These disciplines or any Christian disciplines have no value in themselves. They are not rules to be followed slavishly. It was the Pharisees' outward strictness and inward unyieldingness that provoked Jesus' anger. The purpose of spiritual disciplines is a closer walk with God. The reality and joy of communion with the Living God allows us a freedom from fear and self-interest that is delicious.

JESUS INVITES US

"I have come in order that you might have life—life in all its fullness" (John 10:10b, TEV).

What does full abundant life have to do with Christian spiritual disciplines? Isn't "full, abundant, lively" inconsistent with "discipline, structure, regularity"? Yes and no. Really it is not a case

[4]John A. Sanford, *Dreams, God's Forgotten Language* (New York: J. B. Lippincott Company, 1968).

[5]Richard J. Foster, *Freedom of Simplicity* (New York: Harper & Row, Publishers, Inc., 1981).

of either/or but of both/and, like so much of the Christian life. This and many apparent contradictions in the Christian faith are really paradoxes—statements that appear self-contradictory but on investigation prove essentially true. "The spiritual life proceeds in a kind of trembling certainty that God's truth lies beyond all verities of logic."[6]

More and more I experience life as paradox. There is God and there is Satan. There is light and there is darkness. There is the material world and there is the spiritual world. There is joy and there is sorrow. There is struggle and there is peace and contentment. All these are in the world and they are also within me. I have neither the wisdom to thread my way through the mixture of good and evil I find within and without me, nor the power to effect the changes I want to make within and without me.

Theoretically I have a choice, but realistically, if I am honest with myself, I know I cannot live successfully, I cannot manage on my own. Life is a paradox. Life is a struggle. Life is good even in the struggling; the alternative is death. Only through the reconciling power of the Holy Spirit can I find my way and make my choices. I choose to "remain in the Vine." I don't want to wither. I want to bear fruit. I want my life to have meaning.

"TASTE AND SEE" SUGGESTIONS
Exploratory Steps in Finding Your Way of Spiritual Growth

1. Using paper and pencil, list on the left side of your paper all the disciplines you practice regularly or occasionally in daily living (eating, jogging, attending worship, etc.). Across from each write the benefit you derive from keeping the discipline. Is time alone with God on your list? How do you feel about that?

2. Can you remember any "amazing grace" experiences you have received from another person—times when you deserved and expected a reprimand, but instead were met with love and acceptance and no mention (verbal or nonverbal) of your faults?

3. Treat yourself to a bunch of grapes. Savor them. Empty yourself of all thoughts, feeling, desires, except to enjoy and "be." Open yourself to the possibility that God may speak to you through those grapes.

4. Read Abram and Sarah's story in Genesis 12–24.

5. Most of us feel more comfortable being part of the majority, yet being faithful disciples today can put us in a minority position as it did Jesus' original disciples. When and where do you feel part of the majority? The minority?

6. Consider some biblical paradoxes in light of your own experience:

[6]Parker J. Palmer, *The Promise of Paradox* (Notre Dame, Ind.: Ave Maria Press, 1980), p. 20.

And Jesus concluded, "So those who are last will be first, and those who are first will be last" (Matthew 20:16, TEV).

"For whoever wants to save his own life will lose it; but whoever loses his life for me and for the gospel will save it" (Mark 8:35, TEV).

"Whoever does not take up his cross and follow in my steps is not fit to be my disciple" (Matthew 10:38, TEV) and "For the yoke I will give you is easy, and the load I will put on you is light" (Matthew 11:30, TEV).

7. Learn this song. Sing it often.

I AM THE VINE

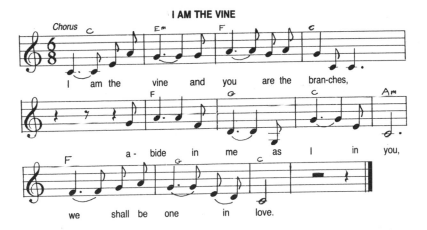

© 1968, Shawn Tracy, OSA, from the album *HARVEST, He Shall Be Peace.*

2

Meditation: Opening Up to God

Tilden Edwards tells of a religion instructor in a Christian high school who gradually introduced silent meditation to his students at the beginning of class until they practiced meditation for ten minutes every day. The instructions were "simply to 'be' during the silence: to be relaxed and awake, open to life as it is, with nothing to do but appreciate whatever comes."[1] The students' response was enthusiastic; they valued the only time in the day when they were not expected to achieve. Some parents, though, were irate over paying tuition for their children to sit and do nothing. Edwards then asks, "How is it that ten minutes of silence can be so special and so threatening?" His answer is that the students appreciated the basic life rhythm of silence and work that was misunderstood by and threatening to their parents.

RECLAIMING OUR HERITAGE

It is sad, but true, that today most Christians are unaware of how to practice and benefit from Christian meditation. They don't understood what meditation is. And what we do not understand is often threatening and suspect. The church continues to offer worship, prayer, study, and service as resources for growth and abundant living, but for the most part has let meditation fall by the wayside. Silence and stillness are hard to come by anywhere these days, even in church. This is so consistently true that when young people or harried, tense persons of any age recognize their need for meditation, they often turn to Transcendental Meditation or Eastern religions and gurus, not to the church.

"Reaching into the silence to experience the presence of God is not new in Christianity. Our heritage, from its beginnings in the Jewish religion, has always acknowledged silence as a way to realization of God's presence."[2] Many passages of the Old Testa-

[1]Tilden Edwards, *Spiritual Friend* (New York: Paulist Press, 1980), p. 69.
[2]Fay Conlee Oliver, *Christian Growth Through Meditation* (Valley Forge, Pa.: Judson Press, 1976), p. 23.

ment remind us of the link between quiet and knowing God, such as:

> But they who wait for the LORD shall renew their strength,
> They shall mount up with wings like eagles,
> They shall run and not be weary, they shall walk and not faint.
> Listen to me in silence. . . .
>
> —Isaiah 40:31-41:1, RSV

Jesus followed that tradition. We often read, as in Mark 1:35, of his rising early to pray in solitude. If we accept Jesus' call to discipleship "Follow me," that includes following into times of refreshment with our Parent as well as into service in the world. In practical terms we will "burn out" trying to do it all without the comfort, guidance, and power of the Holy Spirit. Grapes need a Vine.

Again and again God uses a remnant, a minority, to preserve what is important. So it is that from Jesus' time until the present, mystics—those who experience God directly, who know they are in mystical union with Christ—have kept alive the tradition of meditation. Paul knew he was an apostle because the risen Christ confronted him. He wrote often about being "in Christ." Augustine, Francis of Assisi, Catherine of Siena, Ignatius of Loyola, Theresa of Avila, Meister Eckhart, Brother Lawrence, Evelyn Underhill, George Fox, Frank Laubach, and others are known for their meditative practices that sustained their servant life-styles. Just as important are the unknown faithful who daily live(d) out, "Pause a while and know that I am God, exalted among the nations, exalted over the earth!" (Psalm 46:10, Jerusalem). So our course has been well charted. We need only consult their maps (writings) and get on board if we want the inner journey of meditation. We are simply recovering our Judeo-Christian heritage that many have bypassed.

EXACTLY WHAT IS IT AND WHAT IS IT FOR?

The word "meditation" is commonly used by Christians and non-Christians to describe a wide variety of practices, but all meanings include some connotation of quiet or stillness. In this book, "meditation" refers to a practice used to clear our minds and quiet our hearts in order to create a dwelling place within for the Most High. "The Christian may believe firmly in his or her spiritual nature, but may not always know how to realize it consciously so that his or her total life can be lived abundantly. Meditation is a tool for developing a new state of awareness or consciousness. For the Christian, it can be a pathway toward greater awareness of his or her inner self, his or her spritual being"[3]

[3]*Ibid.*, p. 15.

It is the opposite of thinking about something, deciding what to do, trying to solve a problem, remembering—which are the common uses of our minds. (However, we may do all these things better *after* a meditation time.) Instead of filling ourselves with information and intentions, we empty ourselves to prepare room for Christ. Meditation is a letting go of our usual thoughts and feelings so that we can be more aware of God. Most of our lives are lived in the conscious world with our ego in control. Meditation is a way to shift toward the unconscious, another level of awareness, where it is possible to experience unity with God.

> Meditation, especially as practiced by Christians, is only a means to an end. Although enjoyable in itself, it is not for the purpose of experiencing some kind of psychic high, akin to drug use. Although various degrees of relaxation and sensation are realized, and levels of ecstasy are sometimes experienced, the meditation experience itself is not the reason for practicing it. *The important change is in the lives of the persons meditating.* Persons who meditate regularly day after day will find several things beginning to happen. Their days will become more efficient and productive. Their purposes will become clearer. The work that they want to do, they will do more easily. They will gain a sense of peace in their daily lives and will find their interest in spiritual things growing. The purposes of their lives may change in accordance with new spiritual insights. *They will find an increasing ability to love*[4] (italics added).

A SPECIAL PLACE

When I was a child we regularly visited my great-aunts in an old farmhouse. Usually we went on Friday evening and gathered in the kitchen near the wood stove. But occasionally we went on Sunday and then we sat in the large parlor, used only on Sundays or very special occasions. This may seem only a quaint custom from another era. Yet a Sunday parlor kind of place, free of workday associations is ideal for spending some sabbath time in meditation. Where can you find a special place?

You might be fortunate enough to have a church nearby that has an open chapel for meditation, but most of us are going to have to find a place in our house or apartment. Except for those who live alone, real logistical challenges confront us. We may even be uncomfortable about acknowledging our need for quiet to other members of our household. Will they think us weird? We may feel that if we start and fail, our weakness will be exposed. Still, nothing ventured, nothing gained; so choose an appealing spot and a quiet time of day or night that is prime time for you. I like being by a window that gets the morning sun. Placing a lighted candle, a growing plant, a lovely picture, or an art or nature object near

[4]*Ibid.,* p. 19.

you may give an ordinary place a "Sunday parlor" atmosphere. Or you may prefer just the opposite: the plainest, barest spot may be the least distracting. During nice weather nature lovers may like a lovely spot in the woods, by some water, a garden setting, a hilltop, or a desert vista. Finding your right space and place may not be easy, but it is possible. Bring your desire for intimacy to God and pray for grace and guidance. Once you have found your special place, stick to it. Keeping the same time and place regularly is important in establishing helpful associations.

SOME BASIC GUIDELINES

A *short prayer* to focus attention on your purpose and to ask God's blessing on your efforts is a helpful prelude to meditation. Scripture, such as "Create a pure heart in me, O God, and give me a new and steadfast spirit" (Psalm 51:10, NEB), is one possibility.

Body language is an important form of communication. Our body stance reveals our attitude. In meditation we are seeking to be open to God, so having our hands in a palms-up position is appropriate. Either closing our eyes to keep out all visual distractions or focusing on one selected object will facilitate our singleness of purpose. A relaxed but alert body is ready to receive.

Especially if we meditate in the middle or end of a busy day, our bodies are likely to be holding much accumulated tension. Stretching or tensing then letting go each body part individually from toes to eyeballs is a valuable relaxation technique. It is an application of the physics law that for each action there is an opposite and equal reaction. Deliberately tightening a muscle sets it up for relaxing it. Rigid, "up-tight" bodies are barriers to the Spirit.

Since we are body and mind and spirit—distinct but inseparable, a human trinity—preparing our body is an important beginning stage. Sitting in a comfortable chair with a straight back, feet flat on the floor, is a common meditation posture. Lying on the floor on your back, legs slightly apart and arms a little away from your body is also often used. Sitting on the floor or a low stool with your legs crossed and close to the body, with an erect spine, is a more classic pose, but less comfortable for many beginners. Only you know what feels right for you. Good posture combines balance and comfort.

Breathing, of course, is necessary for life. Deep breathing which fills the abdomen, the diaphragm, and the lungs, buoys and energizes us with increased oxygen and gives us an internal massage. "For the Christian correct breathing should be an important matter, for when God first created man He 'breathed into his nostrils the breath of life; and man became a living soul' (Genesis 2:7,

KJV). The word there for 'breath' is the Hebrew *ruach,* used in Scripture for the Holy Spirit. It seems, then, that when man was created his breath had a twofold connection: with his physical and with his spiritual life. Since man was created 'in the image' of God, this inbreathing by Almighty God is significant."[5] Although there are various specific breathing exercises, all of them emphasize deep breathing from the abdomen, holding the breath several counts, and then exhaling—all done slowly and rhythmically. Deep breathing can be accompanied by counting your breaths, saying a word or phrase such as "Jesus" or "I Am" or silently remembering the words of a hymn like "Breathe on Me, Breath of God." This attention to our breathing is done to bring our breath or spirit into closer harmony with God's Breath or Spirit.

Being in the silence with God, alertly listening to hear God speak, is the chief purpose of meditation. The invitational prayer, body relaxation, and deep breathing are all preparation for this coming home to God. If thoughts or anxieties pop up, just watch them go by. When you notice noise or other distractions, calmly ignore them. This time is for you and God alone. Don't try too hard. Be passive. Allow any images or words that form deep within you. Be attentive to the Inner Light. If you begin with three to five minutes of silence, you may gradually increase it to fifteen or thirty minutes. You will probably have varying degrees of success. Be patient with yourself.

Gently *end this time with a "thank you"* prayer. Return to your normal activity slowly. The transition between different levels of consciousness takes time. One beginning meditator found an immediate beneficial carry-over into her whole day: an increased willingness and ability to do one thing at a time.

Appendix A contains a meditation exercise which includes all the elements just described. In a meditation group the material can be read aloud by the leader. For individual use, make your own tape of the material. Since I find meditation and clock-watching incompatible, I tape ten or more minutes of silence and include Scripture and/or prayer both before and after the silent period.

MORE SPECIFICALLY, TRY THESE . . .

Since God is Creator and Infinite, so are the ways of meditation, of creatively opening inner windows toward Love. The following suggestions, limited by space and my experience, are only that: suggestions. My hope is that they help you on *your* way. There is no one right path for everyone. The suggestions which follow are beginning steps that take three to fifteen minutes. They can be

[5]Eric W. Hayden, *Everyday Yoga for Christians* (Valley Forge: Judson Press, 1966), p. 22.

the "centering" or opening of a daily quiet time, followed by other disciplines, or they may be the entirety of your time alone if you are just starting your intentional inner journey.

1. *Body Relaxing Motions.* Sit in a chair with a straight back, feet on the floor, to move toward "relaxed awareness," which is Gerald May's description of meditation. Many of us carry our tension in our shoulders and neck. Tense your shoulders by hunching them and then letting go. Do this three or four times. Drop your chin on your chest. Tilt your head back. Repeat. Drop your chin forward and slowly roll your head in a complete circle to the right. Do the same in a leftward direction. Let go.

Clench your fists as you name each worry and concern you are carrying. Then open your hands and drop your concern into Jesus' hands, or nail it on the cross with a hammering motion, or throw it into the Jordan River. After physically ridding yourself of each worry, sit with your hands outstretched, palms up, to receive God's gifts of love, joy, peace—name what you want.

2. *Nature Lead-Ins.* "The works of Yahweh are sublime, those who delight in them are right to fix their eyes on them" (Psalm 111:2, Jerusalem). Focus on whatever in nature delights you—a cloud, lichen, seashell, insect, spiderweb, tomato, rose, tree, feather, moon, ocean, grass . . . just enjoy. Appreciate. Sit with your chosen gift of nature and let it speak to you of the Creator. Or just sit and feel the bonds between you and all of creation. Allow any thoughts or associations to surface. If one pulls you, follow its leading. Or just let each idea or feeling float by you; notice it but remain detached.

3. *Imaging with Scripture.* Choose an event from the Bible. Using imagination and all your senses, live into it. Decide the time of year and weather. Feel the wind, or mist, or sun. Look into the faces of people. Share their joy, or poverty, or hunger, or sickness, or grief, or excitement. Eat with them. Taste the dryness of the bread. Smell the earth, the flowers, the sea, the animals. Touch the homespun clothes, a shaggy donkey, a wooden boat. Listen to the sounds of children playing, the competition of merchants, the hush when Jesus speaks. Perhaps you will dare to speak to one of them, and fill in some details that are not recorded. This is not the time for study, but rather a time to experience the oneness of the human family across the ages and perhaps to know Jesus more intimately. (More about this in the Bible chapter.)

4. *Being with Jesus.* Imagine yourself with Jesus, just the two of you, in a lovely spot. Choose your favorite setting: walking in the woods, by the ocean, sitting in a garden or by a lake. Just be with him for awhile, not talking but enjoying his company. Feel his arm around you, or match your gait to his. Pick a flower to

give him—or does he hand one to you? If a question comes that you want to ask him, do, and listen for his answer. Any subject is okay. Nothing is off limits. He knows and understands and accepts everything about you. Share your problems. Share your joys. Listen as he tells you how special you are, how much you are loved. As you leave, thank him and promise to meet again soon.

5. *Create Your Own Ritual and Setting.* Gather a few lovely things to make a home worship center or beauty spot. Most of us respond to the beauty and symbolism of candles. Using scented ones or incense may add another dimension. Decide on your symbolism for the number of candles: perhaps one for the unity of all creation, or the one true God; two for the divine and the human; three for the Father, Son, and Holy Spirit. At different seasons add a picture, or art object, or plant, a fabric—whatever seems right to you. Decide on a ritual sequence such as: light the candles, read a psalm (such as Psalm 100), or a favorite word of Jesus, spend time in silence, end with the Lord's Prayer, a portion from John Baillie's *A Diary of Private Prayer, The Book of Common Prayer,* or a prayer from a devotional booklet. You might play recorded music, listen to a tape of your church choir, or sing a favorite hymn. Ritual, symbolism, and beauty call forth our associations with the holy.

6. *Working/Playing with Clay.* Real clay is of the earth—basic stuff—and working with the earth can be a very good way to get in touch with The Ground of All Being. You need to get over two things: the messiness of the clay and the notion that you are supposed to make something realistic. You will need to detach your "mind" from your hands. Just let them play around with the clay, pushing, pulling, squeezing, patting, doing whatever they want to do. Let them get direction from your Center. You are creating your own symbol for the particular time and place you are. Sometimes you smash it and start over again. When you are finished, you will know. I had a very powerful experience while working with clay in which I discovered I had created the same symbol that had been in a dream six months before. I felt that God wanted to underline that dream, to make sure I paid attention.

HALF STEPS

After hearing me talk for months about daily meditation time, a friend finally ventured, "Your first steps are too hard. Don't you have any half steps?" I pondered this a long time and answered, "Yes, but you may be doing them already and not giving yourself credit." You might call them informal meditation. They are in the tradition of "sermons in stones" and "acres of diamonds in your own backyard." "Half steps" are when you don't set aside special time, but do sense God's presence during everyday activities.

Brother Lawrence talked about praying as well in the kitchen with his pots and pans, as in the chapel.

There are the "suddenly aware," the "a-ha-a-a" times—a brilliant sunset, the innocence of a child, a bird's song, a snowcapped mountain, the warmth of sharing with a special friend—when we spontaneously know that God is present. I suspect joggers and other athletes who respect and tune their bodies to rhythmic working condition experience an at-One-ness. Perhaps it comes as they get their "second wind" or *pneuma* or Spirit. For me it comes in very prosaic activities, such as picking cucumbers. During the season I go out to our few plants every morning and find six, ten, fifteen cucumbers. I pick every ripe one, and the next morning I find just as many, and the next, and the next. One day it came to me, "Cucumbers are like God's love—there is always more."

With just a little effort we can use the routine times in our outer lives to focus on corresponding inner issues. When we are cleaning any thing—teeth, golf clubs, dishes, rainspouts—we can reflect on what needs cleaning in our lives. While reading the newspaper, consider where Jesus stands regarding particular issues. What would he say? What would he do? When we wait in line we might ponder what it means "to wait on the Lord." Even driving, with the inevitable traffic lights, could start us thinking of the Christian psychology of color: green associated with the procreative power of the Holy Spirit; red for lifeblood, passion. When we stop for gasoline we could ask ourselves where we are filling up for the inner journey. List the routine times in your schedule and brainstorm how you can connect them with an inner inventory.

Another type of "half step" could be the *little* choices we make. We decide to read a meaningful book instead of turning on TV. We utilize spare moments to memorize a psalm we have copied on a card and carry with us. We give high priority to a ten-minute meditative walk after dinner each evening.

CAUTION: HANDLE WITH CHRIST

A personal encounter with the Living God is the most exciting thing I know of, but like most exciting things, there is an element of danger. The Bible speaks of God and Satan, the Holy Spirit and evil spirits, angels and demons, light and darkness. The Bible speaks truth. There is no guarantee when we open ourselves to the spiritual world that we will meet only God. We may meet evil. Jesus did, in his forty days of meditation before beginning his public ministry. He dialogued with Satan, which is a way of dealing with evil that I will say more about in the chapter on keeping a journal.

As children we were closer to our personified fears—dragons, witches, giants. Then we experienced these as real, despite parental assurances that they were "only pretend." With maturity and intellectual learning we banished these from our consciousness. They may reappear in our meditation in different forms, but with the same *emotional intensity*. What we *feel* is reality for us, regardless of all the rational reassurance we or others heap on us. When these evil images assail us, a simple effective protection is to visualize the risen Christ surrounding and overcoming the evil, along with a verbal prayer to free us from this satanic force.

Over all, our Christian orientation in regard to meditation both determines our purpose and safeguards against harmful aspects. Three precepts are important: (1) Know yourself. Understand why you are meditating. A hunger for God, not mere game playing or idle curiosity, is necessary. Motivation like that of the psalmist is basic, "As a deer longs for a stream of cool water, so I long for you, O God, I thirst for you, the living God" (Psalm 42:1, 2a, TEV). (2) Know that Jesus Christ in his death and resurrection has conquered evil. At the center of the universe, of all our experience, is Love. (3) Know that the inner journey is only part of life. The authentic inner journey always leads us to our outer journey, our ministry in the world. During times of inner struggle it is very important to continue functioning in routine ways and constantly to be in caring human relationships.

LIKE PETER

It is both appealing and scary to be one of Jesus' close followers. Peter is not the only ambivalent one, proclaiming his faithfulness unto death and then denying he ever knew Jesus, all in one evening. A certain amount of fickleness seems to be part of human nature. We sometimes hunger to know God and at other times could not care less—with a full range of ambivalences in between. Obviously we cannot depend on our feelings if we intend to establish a discipline of meditation. The remedy is to pray for the desire to meditate. Unless we pray for this grace, we will almost certainly fall by the wayside sooner or later.

What if you try meditating and nothing happens? Nothing, except you feel cheated or foolish or stupid. Okay. That's a way to be. The disciples felt that way when they could not drive the evil spirit out of the disturbed man. So did Peter; often, I suspect, because he did so many dumb, impulsive things. But Jesus saw Peter's potential, and eventually Peter became stable and mature. Know that God is pleased just because you tried. You are loved and accepted—just the way you are.

The discipline of meditation comes in taking time to be open to God *so God can grace us*. No Christian discipline is ever an end in itself. All the methods are simply ways of letting your body, mind, and spirit return (as muscles are wont to return to their natural relaxed state) to our Source. Be gentle with yourself. Allow.

Finally, remember that the proof of the pudding is in the eating. The proof of your meditation is in your relaxed awareness *all day*. Don't expect mystical-union-with-God experiences often. More often God sends very mundane messages. Christianity is a very down-to-earth religion. One couple, happy together but with the common communication problems of many marriages, participated in a guided meditation experience together. At the conclusion each meditator asked God for an individual word. The husband, who was not the best listener, heard the word "ear." The wife, who often felt exasperated, was given the word "patience." God knows. Trust Love.

"TASTE AND SEE" SUGGESTIONS
Exploratory Steps in Finding Your Way of Spiritual Growth

1. Respond to Psalm 1 personally. For you, is meditating on the law of the Lord day and night hyperbole? Honest desire? Realistic? How about 15 minutes per day?

2. Consider John's vision recorded in Revelation 1:9-19. Have you had any visions? Do you want any? George Bernard Shaw in his play *Saint Joan* has Joan of Arc reply to those who say her voices are only imagination, "Of course. That is how the messages of God come to us." Do you value imagination?

3. Try this "what to do" from Sean Caulfield's *The Experience of Praying:*

> *"Sit with God as you might with the ocean.*
> *You bring nothing to the ocean, yet it changes you.*
> *Or sit with God as you might with your health.*
> *If you are healthy you receive no special messages*
>   *from your internal organs . . . there is simply*
>   *a harmony of togetherness.*
> *Let go of all and go out to All.*
> *Let the Mystery empty you from within.*
> *Surrender your life in faith to his silent presence.*
> *Be silent."* [6]

4. Act on the hypothesis that God wants to spend time with you alone the next time you cannot sleep. Get up, look through the Psalms until you find one that speaks for/to you. Enjoy the stillness of the night as a gift.

5. Treat yourself to a retreat. If you are not aware of a group that offers silent retreats, ask around in other churches, including

[6] Sean Caulfield, *The Experience of Praying* (New York: Paulist Press, 1980), pp. 7-8.

Roman Catholic churches. Or write Dayspring Retreat Center, 11301 Neelsville Church Road, Germantown, MD 20874, for its schedule.

6. Have you had any teachers, like those mentioned at the beginning of this chapter, who encouraged you to try new behaviors and let you experiment on your own with minimal directions? What do you like and not like about this way of learning?

7. Reflect on the difference between knowing God and knowing about God.

3

Prayer:
An Intimate Conversation

In meditation we set the mood and open ourselves to God, to Love. In prayer the conversation begins. We talk and God listens; then God talks and we listen—or vice versa. I was surprised to find that my dictionary first listed an archaic definition of conversation: "an abiding." Prayer is a conversation where we stay with God and God stays with us. We are waited for, and we await expectantly. "Abide," used in the King James version of John 15, was later translated "remain," which is where we started in chapter 1, "Remain in the Vine."

Now if all this sounds cyclical and if the distinction between meditation and prayer seems a bit fuzzy, it is. Helpful as words are, they are also inadequate. For to talk (or write) about anything, we must separate it into parts for we can only talk about *one* thing at a given time. Yet we don't experience life that way. Life is connected and intertwined (like those grapevines in chapter 1 and in John 15). One might visualize the overlap and interrelatedness of the chapters in this book something like this:

This particular listing of Christian disciplines is neither exhaustive nor superior to any other. It is simply *a* way, the easiest way for me to write about Christian disciplines because this structure matches my experience. I could argue that prayer includes—or just the opposite, is a part of—meditation, keeping a journal, Bible use, corporate worship. I don't want to argue either side. For me, right now, intimate conversation is the best way to describe my prayer life.

Henri Nouwen says in *Reaching Out*: "What is closest to our person is most difficult to express and explain. . . . While prayer is the expression of a most intimate relationship, it also is the most difficult subject to speak about and becomes easily the subject for trivialities and platitudes. . . . Still, we have to keep speaking about prayer. . . ."[1]

I have struggled to define what is the essence of this intimate running conversation that I have with God. I know it is basic, crucial to who I am. I know it sustains me. I know prayer connects me with the power that changes me—keeps me growing. I know my prayer life is unique because I am unique—I am the only Louise C. Spiker (1927–) that God ever created. Yet what is most individual is also the most universal. I know this is so because I respond so often from my depths to what others writers say about prayer.

Although I feel my novice status acutely, the words of Thomas Merton, contemplative and activist monk, encourage me to share my experience. "One cannot begin to face the real difficulties of the life of prayer and meditation unless one is first perfectly content to be a beginner and really experience himself as one who knows little or nothing, and has a desperate need to learn the bare rudiments. . . . We do not want to be beginners. But let us be convinced of the fact that we will never be anything else but beginners, all our life!"[2]

I CAN SAY ANYTHING

Few verbal prayers of Jesus are recorded. Those that are came at the most stressful times of his life: his aloneness in Gethsemane and his agony on the cross. Both times Jesus used the word "Abba," Aramaic for "Father." Of course—Jesus *is the Son* of God. The significant thing is that Jesus taught his disciples to use the same term in the Lord's Prayer. "This is how you should pray: Our Father in heaven . . ." (Matthew 6:9a, TEV). We are to consider ourselves on the same familiar (family) level as Jesus when praying.

Before anyone reacts negatively to the masculine parent image, it is important to search for the deeper meaning. *Peake's Commentary on the Bible* says that the "Father" image "expresses

[1] Henri J. M. Nouwen, *Reaching Out* (Garden City, New York: Doubleday & Company, Inc., 1975), p. 81.
[2] Thomas Merton, *Contemplative Prayer* (Garden City, New York: Doubleday & Company, Inc., 1971), p. 37.

deepest trust and affection." The Bible was written in a time when the family was the essential basis of society and the father was the head of the family. "Our Father" is Jesus' way of expressing deepest trust and affection. What is your way? It matters not a whit what term you use. It matters tremendously that you know, you feel, you believe that in prayer you are conversing with the most caring, loving One imaginable. That's it! Imagine the best possible Friend—Parent—Christian all rolled up into one and then know that prayer is meeting with Someone better than that!

If you have that level of imagination, you know that you can say *anything*. No subject is off limits. No feeling or thought or act is too offbeat. Your Listener is unshockable, patient, giving, and forgiving to the nth degree. This is bound to be easier if you have had good experiences with parent and other authority figures. I was telling a friend about the good early memories I have of my first two Sunday church school teachers. "Do you know how lucky you are?" she responded. "My first eighteen years were in a church and home where God was a stern judge. It's hard to get over."

Many, many people have memories of early experiences that cripple their prayer life. It doesn't even matter what the actual facts were. If you *feel* your father preferred your brother to you, that second-rate feeling is your reality. Jacob had the same problem, and what a gigantic wrestling match that eventually led to! If you remember yourself as the only one without gold stars because you couldn't memorize Scripture, then that "I'm-not-as-good-as-the-others" feeling is your reality.

Experiencing complete acceptance and understanding when talking with a close friend or pastor may help you let go of inferior feelings. Often a professional therapist is needed to guide us in working through the blocks and repressions that keep us from growing. Many of us think professional counsel is too expensive. We feel we're not worth it—which may be the problem with which we need help. Loving ourselves is exactly what Jesus told us to do: Love your neighbor as *yourself*. Where are your priorities? I like the part of the member's commitment of the Church of the Saviour, Washington, D.C., which reads: "I commit myself, *regardless of the expenditures of time, energy, and money,* to becoming an informed, mature Christian." Real prayer involves being completely open and honest, telling it like it is, to a trusted and affectionate Listener. If anything is keeping you from that kind of conversation, do something about it—no matter what it costs.

Knowing that you can say anything doesn't mean that you have to say *everything*. Jesus cautioned us not to babble, for God already knows what we need. The Benedictine rule says prayers should be intense but brief—very wise advice. Our verbalizing is defi-

nitely for our sake—so that we are clear about who we are, where
we are, and what we want. We can't tell our Loving Parent anything that Parent doesn't know. The model prayer Jesus gave us
is concise, but inclusive. The Lord's Prayer praises God's holiness,
prays for God's will to be done, asks for daily needs, forgiveness,
and protection. The length of the conversation is not important.
The openness of the pray–er is.

The freedom to say anything leads sooner or later to ask for
what we want. A common saying during World War II was, "There
are no atheists in foxholes." Whether a soldier or not, who cannot
remember a desperate situation(s) forcing us to pray for help? "To
entreat; implore" is the most common meaning of "pray" as listed
in the dictionary. That's where most people *are* relative to prayer.
Among churchgoers this often is guilt producing. We wish we had
been on better speaking terms with God before we got ourselves
into the current mess. This situation did not seem to bother Jesus
as much as it does us: "Ask, and it will be given to you; search,
and you will find; knock, and the door will be opened to you. . . .
how much more will your Father in heaven give good things to
those who ask him!" (Matthew 7:7-11, Jerusalem). The balance to
any indiscriminate asking on our part is the authentic caring of
our Loving Parent. God loves us more wisely than we love ourselves. There is security in knowing a loving parent won't hand
us an electric mixer if we're only ready for an egg beater.

THY WILL BE DONE

Telling it like it is to a God who really cares is a great beginning,
but more important is where we are at the end of our prayer. In
Jesus' teaching prayer, the phrase "Thy will be done" follows soon
after "Our Father." At the end of forty days of fasting and struggle
Jesus banished Satan with, "Worship the Lord your God and serve
only him!" (Matthew 4:10b, TEV). In Gethsemane after owning
his distaste of suffering he concluded, ". . . But let it be as you, not
I, would have it" (Mark 14:36b, Jerusalem). In prayer God meets
us where we are, but calls us to more than we are; God calls us
into the coming kingdom way.

Getting from where we *are* to an honest "Thy will be done"
usually seems like a gigantic leap across a very wide chasm, with
no bridge in sight. I'd like to offer a few building materials, a few
clues:

1. *Feeling accepted*. The paradoxical truth is that when we feel
fully accepted as we are, we are freed to change. God does not
"Yes, but you should . . ." us. God says, "I love you just the way
you are." Paul puts it, ". . . it was while we were still sinners that
Christ died for us!" (Romans 5:8b, TEV).

On a very down-to-earth, everyday level, I find Thomas Gordon's "active listening" technique very facilitating of person-to-person communication. Active listening is giving feedback by saying in your own words what you heard another person say, including how you think he or she felt when it was being said. It lets the other person know you are really listening and understand, which is a tremendously affirming experience. After having good listening experiences with people, I understand God better and find it easier to believe I am heard.

When you tell a friend that your throat is getting sore and that your boss chewed you out for something you couldn't help (your battery was dead), hearing, "You ought to find another job," or "I always carry jumper cables in my trunk," or even, "You ought to go to bed early tonight," is no help! It just sounds like advice, judgments, or "I told you so." Whereas, "You really work hard without much appreciation," or "A dead battery is a real bummer," or a sympathetic "I do hope you can treat yourself to a relaxing evening by the fire" lets you know you are heard and understood. Then, in your own way, on your own time, you may decide to be more assertive at work, have your battery checked more often, get to bed earlier or work on whatever solutions seem best to you. You feel free to change because no one told you what to do, but listened and likes you as you are. God is that kind of Listening Friend.

2. *Getting one's own way isn't so great.* The longer I live, the more convinced I become that I don't know what's best for me. I am beginning to listen to myself say "never" so I know what I'll do next. I say things such as: "I'm never going to go to school again," and find myself happily enrolled in a course on the Old Testament prophets.

Often it is a matter of timing. I have learned, am learning, and will continue to learn that God's timing is not my timing. I register for a workshop I'm sure is exactly what I need, but have to cancel due to a family emergency. Later an invitation comes for a repeat workshop which fits my schedule very well. My myopic sight just doesn't compare with God's vista-vision.

It is somewhat comforting to know the disciples had similar problems, wanting to know when the kingdom would come, when God would put everyone and everything in their places. Jesus answered that it was not for them or us to know the times or the seasons. And when the opposition started flexing their muscles during that first Holy Week, the disciples sure "split" in a hurry. It took a death and resurrection before they began to understand that God's way was not their way.

Death is no more appealing to us than to Jesus' disciples. Yet often parts of us need to die before we can experience resurrection, new life. When I consider all the grief I have caused myself and

others by my willfulness and attempted shortcuts, I resolve to
trust God sooner, to move toward "Thy will be done" with more
deliberate speed.

3. *Changing me.* "It's me, it's me, it's me, O Lord, standing in
the need of prayer," sums up an attitude that is willing to work
on getting the log out of my eye rather than pointing at the speck
in another's eye. It is almost unbelievable how much easier it is
to see other people's specks than our own logs—except for the fact,
of course, that we can't see our own eyes without a mirror. That's
what we are doing when we are "bugged" by another's faults—
seeing our shortcoming reflected in him/her. It has little to do with
the quantity or quality of the other's transgressions, but the clue
is our negative reaction to a particular trait. There may be ex-
ceptions to this rule, but every time I think I discover one, time
and a deeper look within prove me wrong.

For instance, Ken is very aloof and never seems to want to talk
with me. It "bugs" me that he never reaches out to me, never
initiates a conversation. I decide Ken is just "stuck-up." If I should
by any outside chance consider Ken prayerfully, it would probably
consist of my asking that he change and be nice to me. On second
thought, or fourth, or tenth, I realize there are people I hurry by
without speaking. I may rationalize that I am intent on my task
or they don't like me, or any number of things, but the fact of the
matter is, *I* am aloof. Ken may also be aloof, and continue to be
aloof, but I no longer feel he is "stuck-up." Now I realize he is shy
or a dreamer or whatever. I may even enjoy reaching out to him,
since I have recognized my aloofness "log" and want to change.
Now my prayer is that I be forgiven and given the courage and
grace to change; this is very different from expecting God to mold
Ken to fit my need. It's me, not the situation or the other person,
but it's me, O Lord, standing in the need of prayer.

Honestly living and praying "Thy will be done" in all circumstances of our daily lives is no easy task, but it is *our task* as Jesus'
disciples. Remembering that prodigals are always welcomed home
and that God cares for us with a loving wisdom far beyond our
limited knowledge can move us from rote prayers to heartfelt
"change me, not them" praying.

INTERCESSION

A church member was attempting to convey her concern to a
young bride who, despite her doctor's best efforts, was still on
crutches a year after a fall. "What can I do for you?" the sympathetic person asked. "Pray," earnestly replied the patient. "But
what can I *do* for you?" repeated her friend, betraying her feelings
about intercessory prayer. The well-wisher is not alone. Few of us

believe or act as if we believed the truth of Frank Laubach's ringing title *Prayer, the Mightiest Force in the World.*

We do not tell God what to do in intercession (or in any kind of prayer). We pray for the person to be open to the love-life-energy of God. We are not praying to persuade God to try harder. We are persuading people to listen to God. If a garage door opens when we push a wireless button in a car, is it so strange that a person opens up to new awareness of God when we focus a loving prayer on him/her? Frank Laubach said we are like telephone operators at a switchboard; we connect God with people and leave the talking to God. He urged that we use flash prayers all day long, wherever we are, finding and using all the little chinks of time. I like to use images as I do this: picturing Christ walking arm in arm with a troubled couple, or gently carrying a tired and aged friend, or being light in a hectic office. Concluding with a "thank you" affirms that I have been heard.

Intercessory prayer is an appropriate way to carry out Jesus' command to love one's neighbor as oneself. As we get our own security off our hands—into God's—we can reach out to others more effectively. A helpful sequence is: (1) meditation, the opening of ourselves so we can hear God's will for us; followed by (2) intercession, including others in our prayer. How dare we ask for God's will in others' lives until we have listened, known, and obeyed God in our own! For me, a constant reading and rereading of the Bible and modern devotional writers is indispensable for sensitizing myself to how God works in and through us humans.

But how do we know for whom to pray when the whole world is needy? Follow your inner promptings, emotions, sense of rightness, "gut feelings," the flow of the Spirit. Jesus was moved with compassion for others. Pray for those who arouse your compassion. If intercession feels like an "ought" or "should," God will probably lead another to pray for that person or situation.

Prayer and action must be partners, or both will be weak. As I have prayed for a loved one, wanting her suffering to be allayed, I have been changed. I realized my motivation was largely that I be spared the pain of watching her suffer. My attitude and priorities changed so I could joyfully spend more time with her. "Bearing one another's burdens" was no longer a phrase, but a reality. I could see her load lighten as I shared it. Our three-way intimacy deepened—God, she, and I.

LISTENING IN SILENCE

"We expect too much from talking, too little from silence," says Henri Nouwen in *The Genesee Diary*. Amen and amen! Except for the Society of Friends' silent meetings for worship and Roman Catholic silent retreats, few contemporary Christians have learned to use silence as a way of listening to God. I have no statistics but my considered judgment is that an overwhelming majority of Christians think of prayer exclusively as verbalizing. Yet the God who spoke to Elijah not in the wind, earthquake or fire, but as a soft whisper of a voice, is still available. Are we?

If Jesus spent forty days alone and we have recorded in the Gospels only three questions and answers from that time, it seems reasonable to assume that there was a lot of silence. Gethsemane included three short sentences during an hour of prayer time. No words are recorded for the other times when Jesus went apart to pray. The evidence points to Jesus' prayers being less taking and more listening. Can we move in that direction?

Silence is necessary for our prayer growth, but it is not easy. Sean Caulfield has written an excellent book, *The Experience of Praying,* in which he shares his growth and insights from spending two years alone in a trailer beyond the Trappist abbey to which he belonged. Trappists practice silence more than most orders do, but Father Caulfield felt he had to be even more alone if he were ever really to learn about prayer. He describes the experience as ". . . 90 percent loneliness and 10 percent a wild mystical joy in the goodness of things. As a relief from being alone I would have welcomed a visit from my bitterest enemy, had I an enemy. . . . But aloneness must become what the word really means—all-oneness with the world, with people and with God."[3] People who find that the easiest way for them to think is to talk might find it hardest. Those who prefer quiet to sort out their thoughts have an advantage. Still, God wants to speak to our total being, not just our minds.

Anyone who attempts intentional solitude is going to experience the desert—a dryness, or emptiness. There is also a dryness in our action-packed lives, but we are usually too busy to notice it—which is precisely why we need to take time out. We need to experience our emptiness, to acknowledge our need for and readiness to receive God.

As light and dark are a part of each twenty-four hours, good and evil are a part of our world, and of us. We, too, need to wrestle with our devils as well as welcome the angels who want to help us. I have found both in the silence.

Silence, listening, solitude—all closely related—are means to an end: loving God and others. "Therefore we must seek out the recreating stillness of solitude if we want to be with others meaningfully. We must seek the fellowship and accountability of others if we want to be alone safely. We must cultivate both if we are to

[3]Sean Caulfield, *The Experience of Praying* (New York: Paulist Press, 1980), pp. 35, 36.

live in obedience. . . . Like Jesus we must go away from people so that we can be truly present when we are with people."[4]

The sequence of meditation-verbalizing-listening lets God have the first and last word, a pattern which certainly has a lot to recommend it: courtesy, logic, submission to God's knowledge and authority. Still, I'm ambivalent about the importance of sequence in many areas of life. Sequence is often overrated, especially regarding the way we learn. And prayer is a learning activity—a growing toward a deeper relationship with God and persons. Intimate friends don't communicate by formula. So, again, I say: Experiment to find your own prayer style, but try to move beyond giving a monologue. The silent joy of just being together may be the best part!

HEARING REPLIES

Listening is one thing. Hearing is another. My deaf mother listens intently, but often hears only noises, not recognizable words. She usually catches the meaning, though, because she wants so much to hear that she uses every available resource: hearing aids, body language, facial expression, memory, imagination, context, lip movements. Hearing God's meaning is something like that. If we want the message enough, we can pay attention to many different sources. Messages may come at any time, not necessarily during the silence, but most likely as a result of it. God's replies may come as:

1. *Ideas, insights, inspirations.* It is exciting to see things in a different light, make a new connection, envision a new project. Enthusiasm erupts easily in me, so I have made it a rule of thumb to wait at least a week before I act on a new idea. I also test it out by talking it over with others.

Still, I make mistakes. A memorable one occurred when I became convinced I was called to become involved in low-cost housing for the poor. In preparation I went to Washington, D.C., to see a housing project firsthand, although I had been asked a few days earlier to write a book for Christian educators. Writing had a rating of about "two" (compared to a "ten" for the housing project) on my personal appeal scale, mainly because I saw no need for another book, but also I had never seriously considered writing. Once in Washington, D.C., I had to use the Metro, a horrendous experience because I could not understand the written directions for buying a ticket from a machine. Suddenly, in a flash of insight, I knew I was needed to write clear, simple directions for teachers. Then a torrent of tears engulfed me as I mourned my dying dream

[4]Richard J. Foster, *Celebration of Discipline* (New York: Harper & Row, Publishers, Inc., 1978), pp. 85, 95.

of working in low-cost housing. When the tears passed, a joyful peace filled me. A stranger on the street said, "My, you have a lovely smile on your face. God bless you." God did, very personally, by making sure I got the right message.

2. *Open doors, closed doors.* I have been a planning, organizing, even a controlling person. I still like to plan and organize my life, but I'm getting better at "hanging loose" and changing plans as I come upon an open door—a job offer, an opportunity for new experience, a promise of friendship—or a closed door—a lease not renewed, a request denied, a friend moves away. A yielding, accepting attitude is slowly replacing some of my control needs as I learn to trust. Hindsight helps me to realize that God has been so very trustworthy. Recognizing God in the events of my life adds the precious qualities of expectancy and security.

3. *People.* I hope that every reader has been the recipient of much Christian love and grace from caring persons. Certainly I have. Often I sense more than coincidence when the phone rings or a letter arrives just when I especially need a loving message. Recently a new friend unexpectedly lent me a book which contained a clue to help unravel a dream that had been confusing me for weeks. We experience other persons as gifts most profoundly when we trust enough to share mutually our lives in an authentic and open manner.

4. *A voice.* Twice I have heard a voice—not a dream, not an image—as I awoke, giving me a short message. Both times have been since I began keeping daily disciplines. One was a warning concerning an event just two days hence. The other was a promise which will comfort me all the days of my life. Both required some reflection before I understood them fully. Both were unexpected and unbidden—they were gifts from God.

5. *Body symptoms.* Recent research linking stress, especially guilt and anger, with physical illness gives much food for thought. I find it instructive to pay attention to physical symptoms of distress and experiment with words and images until they lead me to areas of my life that need healing. An upset stomach sets me wondering about the pace of my life. What am I not taking time to chew over, digest thoroughly? A stiff neck causes me to ponder what I'm refusing to turn to or look at. What am I being rigid about? Hives make me realize something is bugging me, getting under my skin; I'd better discover what it is and deal with it. This is not a substitute for medical expertise, but it is a supplement I value. It seems quite reasonable to me that an incarnational God might send messages via my body as well as through my mind and spirit.

6. *Nature.* The grandeur, intricacy, and overwhelming beauty

of all creation has, does, and will always awe and humble me. Such variety allows for each of us to be spoken to in a personal meaningful way endless times, if we but stop to listen. As a woman, the connection between my body, the moon, and the tides speaks to me powerfully of mysterious oneness. A different kind of insight came as a woman exuberantly dancing on a large grassy field exclaimed, "How extravagant God is! He didn't have to make *all* this grass." Earlier she had shared her difficulty in living with an extravagant husband.

7. *The Bible, of course.* The acknowledged Word of God deserves a full chapter to explore its richness (chapter 5, to be exact). I want to insert a brief note here, though, to share my love of Scripture set to music by the St. Louis Jesuits and the monks of Weston Priory. I listen to their records when I am tired, tense, or in special need of comfort. If I fall asleep I don't mind, since the Word is still being absorbed into my subconscious— ". . . he provides for his beloved as they sleep" (Psalm 127: 2b, Jerusalem).

8. *Dialogue with God.* We can consciously choose to use our imagination to encounter Christ or talk with God. The chapter entitled "Putting Imagination to Work" in Morton Kelsey's *The Other Side of Silence* is an exciting resource, giving this technique a biblical perspective and offering practical how-to information plus examples. I will give an example of Kelsey's method in the next chapter, "Keeping a Journal."

9. *Dreams, a Way to Listen to God.*[5] Appendix B gives a fuller explanation of dreams as the symbolic language of God. My first hint about leaving public school teaching came to me in a dream. Until then I unthinkingly assumed I'd continue teaching until retirement age, yet I left without regrets at the end of the year. Although I have paid attention to my dreams for only five and a half years, now I wouldn't "dream" of missing these coded night letters. I feel I am in good company since all of Paul's decisions, according to Acts, were made on the basis of dreams or visions.

10 . . . 11 . . . 12 . . . God's communication mediums are unlimited. How well do you like surprises . . . and waiting? Conversations with God include both.

THE BOTTOM LINE

When all else fails, when I cannot find either meaningful words or communion in the silence I use the "Jesus prayer": "Lord Jesus Christ, son of the living God, have mercy on me, a sinner." What used to be meaningless repetition has become meaningful petition for me.

[5] Title of a book by Morton Kelsey.

"TASTE AND SEE" SUGGESTIONS
Exploratory Steps in Finding Your Way of Spiritual Growth

1. Remember your earliest prayer experiences, what you were taught by word and/or *example* by parents and church. The unspoken examples are the more powerful source of our learning. Were these consistent with the spoken words given you? What were the positive and negative elements of this early experience?

2. Consider Jesus' practice of thanking God before eating and drinking. Is it your practice? Why, or why not?

3. Try imaging with your intercessory prayer. What do you believe God most wants to give your friend? Rest? Then image Jesus skillfully massaging her/his tired body and keeping watch as your friend sleeps. Self-confidence? Image Jesus beaming at and verbally affirming your friend, walking and talking with him/her. Joy? Image Jesus asking your friend to dance. Do they waltz, square dance, or tango? (I hope these examples spark your imagination!)

4. Reflect on your pattern of silence and speech. In *Celebration of Discipline* Richard Foster considers solitude an outward discipline because it is time spent alone that determines our behavior when with others. The preacher of Ecclesiastes says there is "a time to keep silence and a time to speak" (Ecclesiastes 3:7, RSV). Without time with God it's hard to know when to do which. Do you think your tendency is to speak too much or too little?

5. React to this quote from the article "What Makes Churches Grow?"[6] "The congregation, under his leadership, has established a seven-day-a-week, 24-hour prayer group—100 people who have committed themselves to one hour daily of intercessory prayer." Would you want to be in a church like that? What do and what don't you like about it?

6. Imagine what it would be like to take a ten-minute silent prayer time when there is a difference of opinion in your family or church meeting. Do you have that much imagination? Quaker families and Quaker meetings find this practice helpful and workable. All decisons are based on "the sense of the meeting"—there are no majority rulings. During one heated discussion where there were sharp differences of opinion, one Quaker prayed aloud, "O Lord, help us, we're in a fix." After ten minutes of silence during which each Quaker individually searched and listened for God's will, a new spirit (Spirit) pervaded and a decision was quickly and amicably reached. If unanimity does not grow out of the time of silence, there is enough affection, respect, and trust within the body that a small minority is willing not to stand in the way.

7. Flash intercessory prayers as your compassion suggests while reading the newspaper or listening to TV news.

[6] Mary Anne Forehand, "What Makes Churches Grow?" *The American Baptist*, March, 1981, pp. 11-14.

4

Keeping a Journal:
Honest to God

A journal is a personal record of feelings, thoughts, concerns, and visions, often written as letters to God. Journal writing is a way of capturing the inner person to gain self-understanding. It includes any and every part of life, but is more concerned with meaning than with events, especially ultimate meaning. I resonate with the young man who wrote, "I began journaling in my freshman year of college, and I am now in my seventh year of that habit, which is really a blessing. My journal is full of banality and poignancy, gaps of a month or more, my love life, and my walk with God all mixed together. It began as the record of my inductive Bible studies, and while it has deviated from being solely meditations on Scripture, the connection is still strong. It also includes several crucial prayers which still serve as milestones and guideposts for me. It is a tangible record for me, even when my feelings are otherwise, of God's faithfulness to me, and of my involvement with Him."[1]

TALKING ON PAPER

All writing is just talking, put on paper. Many times we are not sure what we think until we say it. When our thoughts, and especially our feelings, reveal our inner selves it is harder to own them, to say them even to a close friend. That is where a journal comes in. It is a safe place to face the parts of ourselves that we don't share anywhere else.

Sometimes I am so full of concerns and feelings that the words gush out and I just catch them on the page. It is a relief to have them outside me where they are easier to see and deal with separately. At such times writing in my journal becomes a release, similar to tears. And as my tears leave me cleansed and ready to be met, because I have let go of the blocks between God and me, so my journal writing opens and prepares me to meet God. I don't

[1] From the spiritual autobiography of Greg Ikehara-Martin.

meet God when I pretend, especially when I pretend I have only positive feelings.

At other times I need to ask myself questions: What is going on in my life? How am I really feeling? What do I like, not like about _____? What's the worst thing that could happen? What do I need to let go of? Or as John Wesley used to ask, "How goes it with your (my) soul?" My journal receives honest answers.

NOTHING BUT THE TRUTH

Writing in a journal or keeping a journal is a method that facilitates my taking the time and effort to be honest with myself before God. There is no rational reason why the same thing couldn't be done by thinking or meditating or talking out loud, except that none of those works as well for me as writing in my journal does. I have a friend who talks aloud as she walks around the house, saying the kinds of things I write in my journal. Another friend writes me a letter using a carbon to copy it in her journal because just writing in her journal is too impersonal. She wants a real person on the other end. *Honesty,* not writing, is the large issue, so even if you abhor writing, please risk reading further to see if any of the process meets your need.

Despite the lip service we render to honesty, few if any of us are always completely honest with ourselves or others, especially in the area of our feelings. We tell "little white lies" or choose not to speak up for at least two reasons: One, while there is a general acknowledgement that we are all sinners, there is an overriding expectation that we be good Christians, or at least nice people. This does not give us permission to be jealous, greedy, angry, scared, or to have any other "negative" feeling. Two, since most of us are kin to Charlie Brown with his "I-need-all-the-friends-I-can-get" cry, we become very adept at hiding all these unacceptable feelings, not only from others, but from ourselves. We are afraid others will think less of us if they know our weaknesses. We repress them without realizing we are being dishonest with ourselves and with God.

Writing in my journal is a prayer form for me. "Prayer becomes attention to *presence*—not only God's, but one's own. . . . The transcendent, which we so neglect and for which we have such deep yearning, is not only where God lives, but where *we* live when we are most alive. Our commitment to the transcendent is the refusal to allow the best years of our lives to happen without us."[2] Focusing on myself, on my many selves, is not narcissistic. I am not staring at my own image but being intentional about my search for the

[2]James Carrol, *A Terrible Beauty* (New York: Newman Press, 1973), pp. 59, 60.

image of God within me. I am digging through my dung to find the gold beneath it. Keeping a journal helps me pay attention to God and to me.

TWO IMPORTANT THINGS

1. *There is no wrong way to keep a journal.* All I have said or will say about my way of keeping a journal is only that: my way, *a* way—not *the* way. Keep your journal any way that helps you be honest to God.
2. *Privacy is essential.* When writing you must feel supremely confident that it is for your eyes alone. You may wish to share portions with a trusted friend, but it must be by *your choice.* Take whatever steps you need—buy a briefcase with a lock, hide it ingeniously, speak of your privacy need to those with whom you live—so that you feel free to write *anything.*

THE COVER AND THE CONTENT

Contrary to all the well-intentioned advice I have received, I buy the thickest and cheapest spiral 8½" x 11" notebook for my journal. Each notebook lasts about a year. The "advice" I've received is to buy either a good quality loose-leaf notebook or a very special bound notebook with a lovely cover. This is meant to remind me that I am worth the very best. I associate loose-leaf notebooks with taking notes from others (professors); keeping a journal is taking notes from myself (an important difference). I like the "special me" concept, but I also like economy. My solution is to redecorate my notebook covers. It takes a month or two of writing in a particular notebook for a personal theme to emerge. Then I use construction paper and markers, gift wrap paper, or a magazine picture to personalize the blah commercial cover. One of my covers says, "It's hard to love people you don't perticlarly like," which is a quote from a child. Another has beautiful butterflies, a resurrection symbol. Currently I am writing between covers showing colorful vegetables that speak to me of ordinary, garden-variety, everyday growth.

My journal contains a record of my inner life as it connects with my outer life. The two lives are inseparable and interdependent. It is a record of where and how I've been, including a lot of verbiage which is part of the process of my spiritual growth. Following are the various components of my journal, some of which appear every day, others only now and then:

1. *Time and place.* It is important to me to have the date and exact time spent in keeping my daily disciplines. If I "fudge" and write 7–8 A.M. when it was really 7:15–8:00 A.M., I will probably tell less than the whole truth farther down the page too. When I

make a summary every three weeks in preparation for meeting with my spiritual director, I need to be clear about exactly what I did and did not do. Recording the place is only necessary when I am away from home.

2. *Dreams.* I include dreams in my journal, rather than keep a separate dream journal, because I consider them an integral part of my life. I put "D" in the margin beside each recorded dream so that I can locate them quickly when I am looking for a pattern or direction. A sequence of dreams often has a common theme which hindsight makes especially evident. I write whatever interpretation is immediately apparent and leave space to add more as I ponder the dream during the next few days. Dreams appear erratically in my journal, sometimes several a week and sometimes none for several weeks. Some persons prefer to draw dream images in their journals, especially those that were especially vivid.

3. *Scripture.* Always I note the Bible chapter with which I am currently working, along with the learnings, insights, and feelings I discover. I'll say more about Bible use in chapter 5.

4. *Silence.* I record the amount of time spent in silence and what I experienced. Sometimes I have to write "Nothing," but again there are entries like: "Two images: one of me singing, dancing, running, carefree—a happy child free to express myself with my body; the other, a lonely, scared little girl alone hugging herself."

5. *Intercession.* This is a checklist item. The list of people for whom I regularly pray is on a separate card that I keep in my journal. I simply record that I have prayed for particular persons that day.

6. *Feelings, Confession, Dialogue.* The bulk of my journal contains the honest-to-God outpouring of the essence of who I am on any given day. In my journal I dare to look at my light (acceptable) and dark (sinful) selves. My journal is mostly verbal, but some journal keepers make doodle drawings when words don't come easily. Using pastels, crayons, or felt-tip markers to express a mood is a way of defining it. Then it is possible to look at it more objectively and choose to let it go. The remainder of this chapter shares my verbal process and includes examples.

OUR MANY SELVES

When I began keeping daily disciplines I used *Our Many Selves, A Handbook for Self-Discovery,*[3] by Elizabeth O'Connor to begin my self-exploration. It is a valuable resource, but I could not have handled it alone. Judging was so much a part of me that I did not realize how hard I was being on myself. It took many a "You are

[3] Elizabeth O'Connor, *Our Many Selves, A Handbook for Self-Discovery* (New York: Harper & Row, Publishers, Inc., 1971).

okay" and "You are accepted as you are," and finally, bluntly, "Stop judging yourself so harshly," from my spiritual director for me to get the message. I suspect I am not alone in this.

As Christians we know that what we do to the least of our sisters and brothers we do to Jesus, that we are to love our enemy in the name of Christ. Yet we seldom consider that the enemy, as the comic strip character Pogo said, is often *us!* Let us be gentle with ourselves. Let us learn to love our enemies within—our dark selves. We take our cue from Jesus' relationship with Mary Magdalene, Zacchaeus, publicans, and sinners—gracious acceptance of what *is,* coupled with an invitation to change and grow.

Gradually I learned that *none* of my selves is *all* of me. I find a selfish self, but also a giving one; a fearful self, but also a trusting one; and so on. My journal, this chapter, and *Our Many Selves* all have more to say about our shadow side than our light side for a very good reason, explained by author Elizabeth O'Connor:

> The exercises here may seem to emphasize our dark dimensions, but it is in order that light may break and we may be born into freedom and joy. Strangely enough we strengthen love in ourselves when we raise into full consciousness the shadow side of our lives. Conversely, when we keep negative feelings out of sight, they smother the love that seems to lie deeper and closer to the real self. This is probably why there is so much pain in not loving. The life that is not able to express the love which is integral to it grows deformed.[4]

CONFESSION

Much of my journal is confession. When I was introduced to keeping a journal five and a half years ago, I took to it like a duck to water. Now I believe that something deep within me was yearning for a way and a place to confess my sins.

Nothing in my background drew attention to confession. I glibly said in unison with the rest of the congregation, "Forgive us our trespasses as we forgive those who trespass against us," with some sort of unspoken assumption that this was easy, or we were doing it, or that we knew how. None of this was true of me. I had an excellent memory which meant I held onto grudges very well. Actually by praying, "Forgive . . . as I forgive," I was condemning myself. The only structured confession I knew about was that practiced by the Roman Catholic church, and I knew too little to understand and appreciate that tradition. I concentrated on being good, or showing only my good side, so I wouldn't have to confess. When I began journaling, my dark side came into view. I started writing a new more inclusive life chapter, literally and figuratively.

[4]Ibid., Preface xv.

Not surprisingly, I soon discovered my selfishness. How appropriate that my dark side should be visible in the darkness of the night when I couldn't sleep and turned to my journal:

(1:45 A.M., June 16). I am selfish. I have been selfish all my life and I still am. I think of myself first, last, and always—what I want, what I need, how I feel. I don't know how to love S___ because I'm too wrapped up in myself. Nobody seems so important as me. I can't meet his needs because I can't stop thinking of mine. There is no help for me except for you to love me, God, and help me grow up and love. You do love me, I know. Help me feel it. I act out of duty toward C_____ and R_____. I feel lousy about that. I think I am angry way down inside. I think that will have to come out so I can love.

Thank you for opening up next steps for me to take. Please keep the wisdom and courage coming, God. This is not going to be fun or easy.

I was more prophetic than I knew. Not only was it neither fun nor easy, it was painful and took months of work. Spending the necessary time seemed reasonable once I realized I had lived forty-nine years before knowing I was angry—incredible, perhaps, but not uncommon for women of my generation.

(12:00 noon, July 12). So much has been going on in my thoughts and feelings the last couple days. I wish I could open myself up with a zipper to lay it all out easily, instead of having to pull, sort, unravel it bit by bit. I think the most important part has to do with anger. I keep pushing my anger down inside because I'm afraid of letting it out. I can't face the possibility of a fight, that I might hurt or alienate the person I'm angry with. I have no skills, no precedents in this area.

Journaling was not enough. I went to an anger workshop which was both terrible and wonderful, and found out that that is how I am. At this workshop I also found out about pounding pillows— an absolutely marvelous thing to do (in private).

(Anger workshop, 10:15 A.M., September 26). Assignment: Fantasize meeting Jesus. I really can't identify with this. I don't want a fantasy trip with anyone. I want a REAL EXPERIENCE. Real feelings—shouts, cries, tears—whatever is inside that's no good. I want it out! But I want people to accept and understand me. I don't feel that here. I am angry, disappointed. I am selfish—and that feels terrible. I know I'm not listening to others as I should. I just want to be understood.

(12:00 noon). I guess what I've learned is I am judgmental and rigid and I really haven't made much if any progress. I had expectations about this anger workshop. I am not very flexible. I would like to feel forgiveness and acceptance, but I think I am putting road blocks in the way of people and God.

(10:00 P.M., September 27). Elizabeth O'Connor says there is more learning in failure than in success. I have failed in at least part of this anger workshop, but I would like to be more clear about what I have learned.
1) When I am in touch with my feelings I need to own them, not be swayed, hurt, scared by others' responses, especially laughter, but to state where I am and what I need. When I finally did this, it was all okay.
2) I identified strongly with Ann's statement, "I don't like my body controlling me." On reflection, I would like to move beyond that and accept my body, own those feelings, experience them, and then move on.
3) I found myself being judgmental umpteen times—usually areas where I am guilty.

(Home again, 7:15 A.M., September 28). My body is so tired, God. It would just love to sleep and do its thing, but I have a job, a husband, friends. God, help me do the things I must and then rest—relax—let go. Thank you for my weekend, for wonderful people. Help me to learn from it all you want me to learn. I can trust my feelings, my experiencing of You directly. God, You use imperfect people like B_____, D_____ _____ . You can use me. That's Good News! Hallelujah!

Three months later anger was still a huge personal issue. My forty-nine-year backlog had to be dealt with, so I got professional help. Opening up honestly when writing in my journal was good preparation for therapy.

Finally I came to understand the wisdom of Paul's words: "If you become angry, do not let your anger lead you into sin, and do not stay angry all day" (Ephesians 4:26, TEV). The point is to deal with anger promptly. Anger is simply a way to *feel* and *feelings just are*. How we *behave* is a separate thing. We can pound pillows or hit persons. We can spout angry words aloud to others or privately journal even our obscenities. Feeling angry is not sinful. Not dealing with our anger, holding a grudge, is.

In my earlier life I never even got to forgiving myself or being forgiven because I didn't admit my anger. I repressed it, which amounts to dishonesty to myself. Since I come from a background of perfectionism (A is good; A+ is better), learning to forgive myself is a frequent growing point.

CONFESSION VIA DIALOGUE

Time and again honesty brings me to admission of my doubts and fears. It seems so un-American to be powerless. I fight it. Yet nothing ever flows from me until I admit my weakness, my inability, my nothingness, and ask for God's wisdom, strength, and power. It's a tearful process and a dreadful nuisance, but that's the way it is!

Trusting is all we can do—not because trusting is easy or good, but because *not* trusting is impossible. It leaves us with nothing but ourselves, and that's not enough. "But his answer was: 'My grace is all you need, for my power is strongest when you are weak'" (2 Corinthians 12:9, TEV). Working through from my gutter to God's grace sometimes takes the form of a dialogue.

A basic requirement for developing this dialogue is a belief that there is a spiritual world as well as the space-time world we operate in most of the time. To believe in the resurrection, to know that Christ lives, is to know he is available to us whenever we choose to be quiet and become detached from our busyness. While the transition into this spiritual world may seem awkward, I find that within minutes I relax into another reality where the conversation flows. I write in my journal as my words and God's words come to me. Again I refer you to Morton Kelsey's *The Other Side of Silence* for a fuller understanding and description of this practice.

(7:00 A.M., October 4, by the ocean).

ME: My trust level isn't very high. I want signs, like the Old Testament people.

JESUS: Now, Louise, I want to help. What exactly is troubling you? Tell me about it.

ME: I'm not sure. I don't feel as o.k. as I want to. I don't hear from J⸻. I had trouble again relating to P⸻. I feel so hurt, anxious, rejected by E⸻. I want to feel good, feel close to You, to feel some assurance that I'm on the right track. I'm tense and beginning with a headache, but I came to the shore to get in touch with You and find peace and power (maybe) and direction. I don't know, Jesus, I just feel all mixed up.

JESUS: You're okay, Louise. You don't have to be perfect. You don't have to "arrive" at any certain place. It's okay to be where you are now. I love you, Louise. I love you and accept you here, now, always. Rest in my love, Louise.

ME: Thank you, Jesus. I want to do that. How about if I just relax here on the beach and feel the sun as your love penetrating to the innermost parts of me?

JESUS: I think that's a good idea, Louise. Try it.

(11:30 A.M., July 8). I wonder why this ball of fear keeps forming and turning over in my stomach. I ignore it or wish it away, and it goes temporarily but always comes back.

ME: I want to talk to you, Fear. I don't need you. You are blocking me, holding me captive. You are keeping me from being who I really am—who God created me to be. You are keeping me from writing what I need to write, what I am called to say. Get out, out, OUT! I don't want you!

FEAR: You can't get rid of me. I have always been a part of you. I always will be. Fear is part of being human.

ME: Okay. There's some truth in what you say. Fear is part of being human. But I am human, and more than human. I am a child of God. You may be part of me, but you are not all of me. Faith, trust, love are part of me too. You cannot control me. I won't let you. I will put Christ, the Light, the Power, between you and me.

FEAR: I'm shrinking. Christ's Light overwhelms me. I will wait until you need me. Sometimes fear is needed. It isn't good to rush into everything innocently.

ME: True. I need discernment too. Jesus Christ, Son of the Living God, have mercy on me, a sinner.

FINDING IMAGES AND NAMING DEMONS

Many persons find it hard to identify their feelings. Such individuals aren't consciously trying to hide anything from God or evade confession. They just don't know how they feel. Looking closely at ourselves when we perceive that we overreact to any person or event can often lead to self-knowledge, to unmasking our emotions. Images, the products of our imagination, offer clues.

Today, for instance, my mail arrived four hours later than usual. A substitute mail clerk delivered the mail, which explains the delay. I imagined I heard the mail truck eight or ten times and I actually walked out to the empty mailbox five times. Recognizing this as silly, unproductive behavior, I finally asked myself, "Why is that mail truck so important to you? You aren't even expecting a letter from anyone and Monday's mail is almost always junk mail." After a few minutes' reflection I realized that the mail truck was my symbol, my image, for the real world out there. Writing is a very solitary occupation and I frequently have trouble believing there is anyone who wants to read what I am writing. My compulsive, embarrassing ("I hope the neighbors aren't counting my trips") actions called my attention to my doubt and loneliness. My behavior (putting an unreasonable amount of time and energy into "mailbox-ing") did not match my circumstance (not expecting mail). Probing this incongruity, I connected with an image (mail truck) and named my feelings (doubt and loneliness). Naming these demons so that I could pray for power over them brought liberation. Free of "truck sounds," I returned to concentrated writing.

Naming demons and imaging (imagining) are very biblical. The prodigal son "came to his senses" when working on a farm which aroused the image of the farm home he left. All through the Bible the Hebrews and Christians carefully chose appropriate names for places and persons, names which evoked an image about that place or person. Many a psalm begins with the poet naming his fear, anger, or doubt, and ends with his expression of praise, faith, or hope.

For me, confession is more a process than it is the saying of certain words. The process begins as I honestly search for and *name* my demons, which helps me to gain distance from them. This in turn makes it easier to accept their reality because I am less identified with them. Once they are on a page of my journal, I can let go and accept God's forgiveness, paving the way for new behaviors.

In nine New Testament references to forgiveness, the message is the same: Keep forgiving others because God has forgiven you. The way we keep aware of God's forgiveness is through confession. So the way to gain power to forgive others is to confess our sin and receive God's gift of forgiveness through Jesus Christ.

John 20:19-23 tells of Jesus' Easter night appearance to the frightened disciples. The risen Christ showed his scars, gave them peace and his Spirit, and sent them out with authority to forgive and withhold forgiveness. All this was delivered to a bunch of sinners, deserters, men who ran and hid when things got tough! Christ's complete acceptance and forgiveness of their human sinfulness while trusting them with power is a mind-blowing example of how we can be forgiven and learn to accept and forgive each other.

THANKSGIVING

In being honest in my journal I also find my light side, where the goodness of life provided by the grace of God fills me with joy, praise, adoration, and thanksgiving. Alas, I am not a poet and often the best I can do is scrawl several big "thank you"s across the page. I'm pretty big on "Hallelujah" and "Alleluia" too, although I haven't the foggiest notion what the difference is, if any. It is a little less monotonous to use both.

There are many psalms of praise to read and identify with, but sometimes I need to write my own words:

(11:00 A.M., June 3. Dayspring retreat farm.) O God, the sun feels so good and the sound of the wind makes me think of your

Spirit blowing in the world, in our lives, in my life. It's such a neat sound! And colors. I love colors. It must be awful to be color blind. I love the warmth of oranges, yellows, reds, browns. They are related to the earth and the life it gives and supports. But there's something special about the blue sky seen through green leaves or evergreen needles. It's peace and beauty and vastness and God, being larger and greater than human needs. Allelu!

My words are not going to last through the ages in the way that "Bless the Lord, O my soul. O Lord my God, thou art very great; thou art clothed with honour and majesty" and the rest of the words of rhythmic Psalm 104, have. They do satisfy my need to be present to me and my God, to acknowledge my deep feelings of relatedness to God through all the varying circumstances of my life.

Sometimes in the midst of ordinary days I become aware of how good my life is:

(7:00 A.M., March 31). It's good to be alive—to be teaching, to enjoy beautiful warm spring, to love R_____ and be loved, to meet with B_____, V_____, R_____, to know God, to be accepted and loved by God, to feel growth and change is possible. Thanks for life!

Occasionally I have enough ego strength to rejoice in myself:

(8:30 A.M., October 2). I just read back over the last few days. It's been so good, so incredibly good—even the bad parts I did right. I lived into the feelings, worked things through. I hated the pain and love the good feeling afterwards—and I know they must go together. Thank you, THANK YOU, GOD. The celebration was all I hoped for. I can hardly believe it all went so well—and yet, why am I surprised? I know You gave me the idea, and we've been working on it together since last November. THANK YOU AGAIN, LORD!

REFLECTING

Every few weeks it is good to read back in my journal and see where I've been. Often I am pleasantly surprised to realize I have made some progress. Sometimes it is a bit discouraging to note that I sound like a broken record stuck in the same groove, but then I know it is time to give myself a nudge. Summarizing new learnings is one of my favorite things to do. Through it I not only can give myself a pat on the back, but also make my learnings more visible and reinforce my new behaviors.

(7:30 A.M., September 30). Things I wish I had learned sooner:

(1) Life offers many choices and alternatives. For so long I thought there were two ways: the right and wrong, good and bad. Since I couldn't seriously accept myself as bad or wrong, I had no choice!

(2) Confrontation can be good. Peace at any price is too high a price. It's painful and difficult, but change or growth do not come easily or without cost.

(3) Consistency isn't as important as it's cracked up to be. The effort to be consistent can get more like rigidity. It's much more important to be open, honest, growing, changing.

(4) Mistakes are inevitable and natural. Everyone makes mistakes. We are all sinners. It is important to learn to forgive and to be forgiven. This is very hard for me.

Keeping a journal will not produce miracles, but it may help you to be more honest and open toward God's miracle—transformation through the sacrifice of Jesus Christ. We neither have to deserve nor understand this gift of grace in order to receive it. By making honest confession and receiving God's forgiveness we can join the multitudes through the ages who have been changed. Frightened Good Friday disciples met the risen Christ and became fearless apostles.

The disciplines of journal keeping are never an end in themselves. They are always to be the means to put us in a place where we may let in more of God's love, love that casts out fear.

"TASTE AND SEE" SUGGESTIONS
Exploratory Steps in Finding Your Way of Spiritual Growth

1. Remember how you felt about writing assignments in school. Is your attitude toward keeping a journal affected by this?

2. List as many of your "selves" as you can. Do you see an opposite for each, i.e., proud and humble, selfish and generous, etc.?

3. Look up and explore these New Testament references on forgiveness:

Matthew 6:12-15	Luke 17:3	James 5:15, 16, 19, 20
Matthew 18:21-35	Ephesians 4:25-32	1 John 1:9
Mark 11:25	Colossians 3:13	1 John 2:12

5. Deal with your ability or lack thereof to forgive as Jesus did on the cross as he said, "Forgive them, Father! They don't know what they are doing." I find it difficult to forgive those who do not know or will not admit they have wronged me, and very easy to forgive those who sincerely ask for forgiveness.

6. Explore your feelings and behavior in regard to both these

statements: "Honesty is the best policy" and "It's only a little white lie."

7. Show your "scars" to another. Jesus showed his scars to his intimate friends—his disciples—on Easter night. Scars imply a healing. Do you want to share with another how you have been wounded and healed?

5

The Bible
and Other Treasures

A few years ago *Roots,* both the book by Alex Haley and the TV drama, awakened our "melting pot" nation to the value and excitement of knowing our heritage. As we cringed at the cruelty and exulted at the exodus from slavery, we felt our own bound-ness and freedom, regardless of color. Kunta Kinte's story became our story. We sensed the larger sweep of history encompassing our individual lives, explaining, at least in part, the depth of feeling that often clouds and confuses specific situations. One viewer wrote:

> I share the pain of watching *Roots.* I experienced a real sense of God's justice coming about. Alex Haley, on behalf of all his ancestors, is telling the story in such a way as to heal the rootlessness of all kinds of people. Kunta Kinte is free today in Alex Haley. It says to me that justice may not come about in my lifetime but I need to be true to my own call so that I will do my part for the future.[1]

Knowing our connection with the past fills a basic need to feel part of a continuous and continuing family.

Tuning into *Roots* got a lot of people "turned on" to checking out their own roots. At an ethnic and family level many became more enthusiastic about family reunions. Members of the older generation gained recognition for their remembrances of times past. Some people even researched their own genealogy. However, looking through courthouse and library records can consume many hours and appeals to relatively few.

As Christians our faith family is the People of God. Our roots are in the Judeo-Christian tradition. Our story is in the Bible.

Yes, we are a people of the Book, but it is quite possible to reverence the volume without knowing its contents or living its message. Like those motivated by *Roots,* we may have our Bible appetites whetted by a sermon, a gifted teacher or even a TV biblical drama. We turn to the Bible for awhile, either alone or in

[1] From a letter to the author from Judith Roark.

a group (family reunion). Often any formal Bible study is with
someone who has gained recognition (a member of the "older
generation") because he or she knows the family faith history.
Serious searching of the Scripture records to make our own connections is costly in time and energy, so few undertake it and still
fewer stay with it. On the whole, Christians are not deeply rooted
in biblical ground.

FROM CONFUSION TO HOPE

Historians have long claimed that those who do not learn from
the past are doomed to repeat the same mistakes in the future.
Because we are not thoroughly familiar with our biblical history,
we are confused about who we are as a faith community and what
we need to be about as God's people. Confusion begets inertia.
Inertia is the antithesis of purposeful growth and abundant living.
To grow we must constantly struggle with the questions of identity
and life-style which are primary issues in the Old and New Tes-
taments. Without the regular nourishment of Bible reading and
Bible study we remain rootless—and, consequently, fruitless.

Before our faith ancestors entered the Promised Land, God established a covenant relationship with our family. God demanded
first place in the lives of the Chosen People and their constant
attention to God's Word:

> Israel, remember this! The Lord—and the Lord alone—is our God.
> Love the Lord your God with all your heart, with all your soul, and
> with all your strength. Never forget these commands that I am giving
> you today. Teach them to your children. Repeat them when you are
> at home and when you are away, when you are resting and when you
> are working. Tie them on your arms and wear them on your foreheads
> as a reminder. Write them on the doorposts of your house and on your
> gates (Deuteronomy 6:4-9, TEV).

Jesus referred to these verses as the greatest and the first of the
commandments (Matthew 22:37). The only Gospel record we have
of the hidden years between his birth and his ministry concerns
his single-minded desire to learn more: "On the third day they
found him in the Temple, sitting with the Jewish teachers, listening to them and asking questions" (Luke 2:46, TEV). Jesus said
he came to fulfill the law, not do away with it (Luke 16:17).

Paul, the man most responsible for the growth of the Gentile
church, boasted of his training in the law under Gamaliel and
made many references to his Hebrew education in his defenses
when under arrest. Augustine, after living into the pleasures of
this world, made an abrupt about face when he read, "not in
reveling and drunkenness, not in debauchery and licentiousness,
not in quarreling and jealousy. But put on the Lord Jesus Christ,

and make no provision for the flesh, to gratify its desires" (Romans 13:13b-14, RSV). Martin Luther, a professor of theology, launched the Protestant Reformation when Romans 1:16-17 became for him "a gateway to heaven."[2] These few examples are cited to emphasize that there is no getting around the fact that we need to know God's Word if we are serious about doing God's Will.

It is not an arbitrary God who insists that we learn our story and teach it to our children. It is a wise, caring, practical Lord who knows we are confused, ineffective, and powerless without knowledge of the Way. "There is no major issue confronting the modern world that is not addressed in some fashion in the Bible. Solutions to modern problems may not be definitive in the Bible on all counts. But some directive insight is there, and we desperately need to find it. No other community or group is obligated to address issues from any perspective other than its own. Any group can adopt any position on any issue at any time—EXCEPT the Christian community. By our very nature and function we take positions on issues only as we understand biblical insight on the issue. Otherwise we become little more than an echo of secular society. . . . Many *answers* to perplexing problems have been given, but little *hope*. The biblical message embodies hope. We need to hear it—and then proclaim it by living it."[3]

A LIBRARY

Perhaps the biggest obstacle to our spending more time with the Bible is its size. It is *so-o-o* big. It is even longer than a James Michener novel and not nearly as sequential. The reason for this is, of course, that it is not a book, but a sixty-six volume library— a library collected over a span of a thousand years, containing books by many authors who wrote in various places and situations. The Bible contains history, law, drama, poetry, letters, sermons, prophecy, visions, apocalypse (symbolic writing to veil the meaning to outsiders), aphorisms (pithy sayings), and a kind of biography peculiar to the Hebrews, who were not much interested in individuals as such but were very conscious of their nation's special relationship to God.

Yet throughout all the books of the Bible there is just one main purpose: To show how God's prior love has been received in the daily lives of women and men from the times of the ancient Hebrews through the early Christians. The needs and feelings and actions of people then and now are basically the same. The choices, large and small, were no easier then than they are for us. Bible

[2] W. D. Davies, *Invitation to the New Testament* (Garden City, New York: Doubleday & Company, Inc., 1966), pp. 235, 236.

[3] Jan Linn, *Living Out God's Love* (Valley Forge: Judson Press, 1981), pp. 17, 18.

persons were no strangers to mistakes and failures. Persons who think it is only about goody-goodies just have not cracked the Book!

Libraries can be forbidding if we approach them without guidance or understanding of the categories and arrangement of books. Browsing is fun if time is not an issue—but it usually is. Many teachers suggest the best place to begin in the Bible is the New Testament, especially the Gospels, for these tell us of the greatest expression of love, Jesus, who was the Word made flesh.

Although Matthew, Mark, Luke, and John all tell us about Jesus, each writer had his own reason for telling the story. Mark's Gospel is a good book to begin on because it is the shortest gospel and emphasizes the actions of Jesus. Matthew presents much more of the teachings of Jesus and points out his Hebrew roots as well as the branching out of his message to the whole world. The book of Luke is filled with Jesus' concern for the needs of people—all kinds of needs—including the world's need of a Savior. The familiar birth narrative is part of Luke's Gospel, and Luke is also responsible for the birth narrative of the church, the book of Acts. John's is often called the spiritual Gospel because it is concerned with the depth meaning of the events and teachings of Jesus' life and the author uses much symbolism to explain these.

One thing leads to another. Because the Bible is one story, no matter where you start, there are connections or lead-ins to other parts. If you start with one Gospel, you may wish to see how another author tells the Jesus story. Or perhaps you want to know what happened next and go on to Acts which picks up after Jesus' resurrection and ascension. After reading in Acts about the churches started by Paul, his letters to these young congregations may appeal to you. Or reading of either Jesus', Peter's, or Paul's references to the Hebrew law or to Abraham may send you scurrying to the Old Testament to learn more of the early tradition. The references to Jesus fulfilling the Messiah prophecies may lead you to Isaiah and other prophets. And so on.

Another way is to choose books appropriate to your current life situation or interest. Serious illness or misfortune has sent many a person to Job for help with the eternal question of faith and suffering. Realistic, action-oriented types will find many practical instructions in the Letter from James. Those who lean toward the esoteric may like the challenge and mystery of Revelation or Daniel. Either a systematic progression or a follow-your-interest approach can be rewarding. Another option is to take advantage of whatever courses are available in your church school or community. More important than where to begin is *beginning*—actually spending regular intentional time with the Bible.

DEEPER DIFFERENT ROOTS

I have been exposed to the Bible since I was carried to Sunday school as an infant. My associations with the Bible have been positive from the beginning ("Jesus loves me, this I know, for the Bible tells me so" was the first song I learned); yet my experiences were mainly passive and uneventful. I learned mostly through osmosis as I progressed through Sunday school, worship services, and women's meetings. My best times were the many years I taught children in church school because I read and studied the Bible in preparation for class.

Then I discovered the Church of the Saviour, Washington, D.C., where members spend time daily working with Scripture, usually staying with a chapter for one week and working through an entire book this way. Frankly, it sounded slow and strange to me, but the power evident in their lives was so appealing to me that it seemed worth a try. I flirted with this concentrated stick-to-itiveness for over a year, partly out of curiosity and partly out of oughtness, before I settled into a routine practice which I find exciting and rewarding. Now it seems as unthinkable not to develop this kind of biblical root as the opposite seemed earlier. Those who are most familiar with the Bible are usually the most eager to continue to search its richness, which suggests something: Try it. You'll like it!

There are many, many ways to use the Bible, but generally they can be classed under two headings: meditative reading and depth study. These classifications are by no means mutually exclusive but each kind of use has a different emphasis. In meditative reading of the Bible we concentrate on the personal, subjective meaning for us, being as open and imaginative as possible. We are our own authority because we are expecting our own special message to meet our need at the present moment. In depth Bible study we are gathering and analyzing all the relevant information concerning the passage to gain more understanding of the context and content. We need all the help we can get from biblical scholars because the Bible was written in languages, cultures, and times vastly different from our own.

It is definitely another case of both/and, not either/or. The important thing is to broaden your base, to get more firmly rooted in the Bible. Continuing the plant analogy in terms of purpose, we need a long, strong taproot connection to God. We also need many branching roots to reach more of the limitless God of the past, present, and future. So to gather more and more of God's nourishment, we need the long taproot of depth study *and* the supporting branch roots of devotional reading of the Bible. Or maybe it seems the other way around to you. Maybe your taproot is meditational reading but you have branch roots of sustained analytical study. What I am really stressing is the need for *more* and *different* biblical roots, that Christians be continually growing in depth and breadth of biblical knowledge and applied insights.

Reading, meditating on, and studying the Bible do take considerable time and effort, but the results are worth the trouble. We receive an expanding sense of who we are as the people of God and an increasingly clear sense of life direction as our part in God's plan for the Chosen People. Spending as much time daily with the Bible as I do with the newspaper and TV news seems prudent to me. What we spend time with determines what habits we develop. Paul instructed the early church, "In conclusion, my brothers, fill your minds with those things that are good and that deserve praise: things that are true, noble, right, pure, lovely, and honorable. Put into practice what you learned and received from me, both from my words and from my actions. And the God who gives us peace will be with you" (Philippians 4:8, TEV).

RESOURCES FOR BIBLE STUDY

The many versions and translations of the Bible available to us today arc a great blessing. Strange as it may sound to the uninitiated, broadly speaking the newer the translation, the closer to the original text it is likely to be. All original manuscripts are extinct. For fifteen centuries, until the invention of the printing press, the Bible had to be copied by hand; it was incvitable that errors crept in. The discovery of the Dead Sea Scrolls in 1947 and other subsequent findings meant that manuscripts much closer in time to the original ones became available to scholars. Translations since then benefit from these discoveries. Every translator has the problem of differences in thought and language patterns between languages that makes word for word substitution impossible. I am awed, grateful, and somewhat baffled by the painstaking work that these scholars undertake to bring authenticity and illumination to the Scriptures. It seems to me they are working on a gigantic and beautiful picture puzzle, one with some pieces lost and other pieces badly smudged.

Using the fruits of such scholars' labors, different Bible translations and versions, has led me to amazing and even amusing new insights. For instance, I started out looking up a reference to "meditate." My first-used source, the *Revised Standard Version,* indicated that Isaac at the crucial time in his life when he was about to meet Rebekah, his future wife and mother of millions of Jewish descendants, ". . . went out to meditate in the field in the evening" (Genesis 24:63). Next, *Today's English Version* said, "He went out in the early evening to take a walk in the fields," which caused me to affirm taking solitary walks as a way to meditate.

Then I read in *The New English Bible,* "One evening when he had
gone out into the open country hoping to meet them," and I began
to think how human and curious and impatient this forty-year-
old bachelor was. And then I saw this footnote: "hoping . . . them;
or to relieve himself." I quickly reached for my commentaries and
found in the *Jerome Biblical Commentary* that the Hebrew word
lāśûah has been translated both as "to walk" and "to meditate,"
but "More likely . . . the word means "to dig a hole" and is a
euphemism for relieving nature."[4]

This incident delights me and contains a lot of usable everyday
wisdom. Who can deny that each translation has a part of the
truth? We are body ("I gotta go") and mind ("I hope she comes
soon") and spirit ("May Thy will be done in my marriage and in
all my life"). The Bible is an earthy book. It tells of real people
and deals with all parts of life. Yet through all the complexities
and sinfulness and difficulties of living, there is always the assurance that God knows us and loves us and wants communion
with us.

Paraphrases of New Testament books are a good way of capturing the original flavor and excitement of the Good News. Absolute accuracy is sacrificed for a contagious contemporary quality.
I savor the fresh connections I catch from such passages as:

> He left after that, and he saw a Yankee by the name of Levi, working
> for the Internal Revenue Service. And Jesus said to him, "Walk in
> this way with me." He got up, quit his job with the government, and
> started walking in the way with him.
>   And Levi gave a big reception for him at his house. Now there were
> quite a few Yankees and others sitting around with them. And the
> church members and officials said to Jesus' students, "How come you
> all eating and socializing with Yankees and niggers?"
>   Jesus picked it up and told them, "Healthy people don't need a
> doctor—only the sick do. I haven't come to challenge the saved people
> to a new way of walking—only the 'sinners.'"[5]

Paraphrases should be used *in addition to* good translations, not
instead of. They bring a balance to the other-worldly piety we
sometimes confer upon Jesus when reading only classic language.

The articles and maps which appear at the front and back of

[4]Eugene H. Maly, *Genesis, The Jerome Biblical Commentary* (Englewood
Cliffs, N.J.: Prentice-Hall, Inc., 1968), p. 25.

[5]Clarence Jordan, *The Cotton Patch Version of Luke and Acts* (New York:
Association Press, 1969), p. 28. Reprinted from THE COTTON PATCH VER-
SION OF LUKE & ACTS by Clarence Jordan © 1969. By permission of New
Century Publishers, Inc., Piscataway, New Jersey 08854.

Other paraphrases I enjoy using are: *The Gospels* and *Letters to Young
Churches* by J. B. Phillips; *God Is for Real, Man; Treat Me Cool, Lord;* and
God Is Beautiful, Man by Carl F. Burke. These last three are done by kids
from city streets in their own language.

many Bibles, as well as the beginning notes about each book are largely ignored treasures within a treasure. Most readers cannot remember the succession of kings and prophets of the Old Testament, especially during the period of the two kingdoms, but a chronology chart lists it all clearly and in apple-pie order. Who cares? What difference does it make? Well, the difference is something like knowing whether John Adams or Harry Truman was the postwar president mentioned by a particular author in his or her book. Times do change! And who would guess that the Book of Isaiah is really a collection from three different authors writing when Israel was in three vastly different circumstances—pre-invasion, exile, and discouraging post-exile times—without the explanatory notes at the beginning of Isaiah in newer translations? You can't tell a book by its cover, and you can't understand the significance of a writing without knowing the situation, audience, and reason the author was addressing.

I spent $79 during the past year for two different one-volume biblical commentaries. I consider them among the best bargains of my buying career and only wish I had been smart enough to purchase them sooner. They are crammed full of conveniently arranged information. The major part of each is chapter-by-chapter commentary, but there are also many background articles on all kinds of related subjects. They are gold mines—and I own them. Oh, wealthy me!

Geography has always influenced history profoundly, so a knowledge of the climate and topography of Bible lands is important. A Bible atlas fills the bill. After bookstore browsing I chose the one with the most pictures and maps, the largest print, and the brightest colors. It helps me *see* the land. The text in my atlas is a very concise synopsis of the Bible arranged so the connections between story and land are obvious. Geography was never my long suit, but this book hooked me anyway.

Several years ago I took a graduate course in the Old Testament prophets. It cost considerably more than the biblical commentaries, but it was fun and worthwhile. I learned much about the prophets, but I learned more about me. One valuable learning was that if I substitute self-discipline for money, I can learn by reading biblical authorities on my own. I still follow my professor's advice to consult two commentaries. Sitting by my fireplace is cozier than a classroom, but at home I must supply the will power. Choices, always choices.

MEDITATIVE BIBLE READING

For several years my daily Bible time has been a practice of coming with expectancy to the same chapter every day for a week. At the very least, the repetition increases my knowledge of what is in the Bible. But what I most like is the way different stories, verses, or phrases "pop out" at me with personal messages in an unpredictable way.

One of my earliest "a-ha" experiences was when I was working with Luke 8. After a page and a half of nitty gritties in my journal I just gave up trying to sort and describe it all and ended with:

> Confused, muddled. Please help, God. I need grace—acceptance without earning or deserving it. I know you give it, God. Let me feel it.

Then in keeping with my Bible discipline, I reread Luke 8. "The twelve disciples went with him, and so did some women who had been healed of evil spirits and diseases . . ." (Luke 8:1b-2a, TEV). For the first time I saw "disease" as "dis-ease." Somehow, naming my demon, or knowing it had a name, plus acknowledging Jesus' healing power if I went with him, was a tremendously freeing experience. It was one of many times when the linkage between prayer and Scripture was evident. They are an unbeatable combination—a holy duet—pointing the way to the powerful trio— Scripture, prayer, and action—that transforms us and the world.

Recently I discovered that this way of working with the Bible has been practiced by the Benedictines for fifteen centuries and is called *lectio divina*. "The phrase means 'divine reading.' Originally it referred to the contemplative study of the Bible; today it has been expanded to include any book which brings one closer to truth. The vital feature of this discipline is not what one studies but how one studies it. The approach is a slow, thoughtful, prayerful dialogue with the material, grounded in the faith that behind the words we read there is always a Word to encounter."[6]

Having a longtime surface familiarity with many Bible passages has its advantages, of course, but also the disadvantage of a certain "Ho hum, what else is new?" attitude. It was a real breakthrough when I took God's Word seriously enough to react honestly and recorded my anger in my journal:

> Luke 12:33. "Sell all your belongings and give the money to the poor." (In a large angry scrawl) I can't do that! That's too much! I feel angry when I'm asked to do something so difficult and nearly impossible. C'mon, God, can't you see I'm nowhere ready for that? Treat me gently. Take me by stages. Why are you so demanding and hard? NO, GOD, NO! If you demand that, I demand more help, more grace! Help me where I am, God.

I am not proud of the content of my response, but I did respond, which is what God wants of us. Any child knows it is better to be

[6]Parker J. Palmer, *Lectio Divina: Another Way to Learn,* Pendle Hill Bulletin No. 322 (Lebanon, Pa.: Sowers Printing Company, 1978).

paid attention to, even with a spanking, than to be ignored. Whether our response is negative, positive, or vacillating, God's Word always deserves a reading and a reply.

Sometimes I like to look for all the characters in a particular story within myself. Take, for example, the first two chapters of Matthew, the birth narrative. As background, the list of the ancestors of Jesus reminds me of all those persons in my past who nurtured and encouraged me in the faith, from earliest Sunday school teachers to current caring friends in a small group.

Now, what in me, as in Mary, has been conceived by the Holy Spirit, that I can give birth to? A new behavior supporting a minority justice issue? A new simplicity in the way I prepare food, consuming less meat and eating more grains? Or am I birthing a book?

Joseph is easy to find in me. Both he and I want to be known for doing the right thing. No scandal. We preserve our reputations. God does get through to us at night when we are relaxed, through our dreams. Perhaps I, like Joseph, can find the courage to obey God's commands when they come as personal messages.

Certainly I would never give orders to kill all male babies as King Herod did! No, not actually, but there are some male ideas I surely would like to put to death. With word and look I have been known to take deadly aim at those with opposing views.

As the wise men searched for the child, I too search for new gifts within me to offer, new ways to relate, to this Star Child.

Often questions emerge from a week's work with a chapter. The book of Acts always forces me to deal with the vast differences between me and the early Christians. Acts 12 tells of Herod's persecution of early church members, the death of James and the imprisonment of Peter. It was a scary time; I wonder what I would be willing to die for. God's power surpasses Herod's as an angel frees Peter, which is more than Peter is expecting. Hence, I am faced with another question: How much do I expect from God? The issue of the week that emerges as most important is control. What parts of my life does the government control? What parts of my life does God control?

There is nothing special about these particular questions. They just happened to be relevant ones for me one week. *Discover your own questions and live with them.* Neither the questions nor the answers are the most important thing. The struggle and the personal growth that come from real encounter with the Word is what matters.

EQUIPPING THE SAINTS

Verna J. Dozier, a teacher now retired from public school teaching, has developed a manual and tape for self-directed Bible study in lay groups which she calls *Equipping the Saints.* "The point of lay Bible study," says Verna,

> is to help lay people reclaim their authority as the people of God. Even if they consciously reject an authoritarian approach, laity are raised in a culture of dependence on authorities. We're taught to sit at the feet of experts, and not to trust the validity of our own wrestling. . . . Using various translations and commentaries as resources, groups move through three types of questions: 1) What does the passage say? What are the meanings of the words used? 2) What is the significance of the passage? What did it say to the people who preserved it? 3) What does the passage say to me/us now?[7]

These three questions cover both the Bible study and meditative Bible reading aspects previously described.

The Bible was written from a faith community to a faith community, so it is best studied in small groups where each person is a teacher-learner. Truth emerges in wider, deeper, and broader forms as group members share their personal insights as well as the information each has gained from the translation and commentary they have chosen to read. Sequence is very important to Verna Dozier, who feels the background of steps one and two must be acquired before trusting step three.

The designated leader, a role that can rotate among members, functions as a facilitator of group life and learning, not as a fountain of knowledge. This method of Bible study emphasizes *finding our own authority,* both within ourselves (our life experience and our experiencing of the Holy Spirit) and without (listening to fellow learners and to the written words of more advanced Bible scholars).

Finding truth is a lifelong process. Christians need a "hands on" approach, a handling of the Word. Christians must continually seek, and the Bible is a basic source. Working with a group has the advantage of built-in accountability since most of us find it easier to join others in a common task than to be faithful in individual Bible work.

In fact, relying on solitary study has its pitfalls, since we are open to grave errors of misinterpretation without the balance provided by the life experience and study of others. Throughout the centuries the church and the Word have interpreted and balanced each other. Knowing where the portion we are studying fits into the total story is crucial in understanding its full meaning.

[7] Verna J. Dozier, *Equipping the Saints* (Washington, D.C: The Alban Institute, Inc., 1001). Available from The Alban Institute, Inc., Mount St. Alban, Washington, D.C. 20016. A cassette tape by Verna J. Dozier with a synopsis of the "Story of the Bible" on one side and "How to Teach the Bible" on the other is available from Catacomb Cassettes, Episcopal Radio-TV Foundation, Inc., 3379 Peachtree Rd. N.E., Suite 851, Atlanta, GA 30326.

Taking a verse or partial text out of context to prove a point already decided on (proof-texting) can create much evil. We need to pray for an open, questing spirit as we approach the Bible, a readiness to release any preconceived notion or cherished belief so God can do a new thing in us. God's help is necessary because that much openness strains most of us.

OTHER TREASURES

The Bible is *the story,* but we have many more recent ancestors with stories to share and even contemporary cousins who want to tell how it is with them. God and humans have continued to act, react, and interact in the nineteen hundred years since the last Bible book was written. It is not that there are new truths, but there are as many new ways to state old truths as there are lives that have been lived—or are being lived. Often my journal contains comments such as:

(March 23). *The Genesee Diary*[8]—I don't want to put it down. So much speaks to just where I am. P. 59, "Not, 'Do I have time to prepare?' but, 'Do I live in a state of preparedness?'" P. 64, "The most persistent advice of John Eudes in his spiritual direction is to explore the wounds, to pay attention to the feelings, which are often embarrassing and shameful, and follow them to their roots." P. 65, ". . . you will be confronted with your sinful self. This confrontation should not lead to despair but should set you free to receive the compassion of God without whom no healing is possible."

My most dramatic example of being personally addressed by a contemporary author occurred when I read, "At some point, every caregiver must learn to care a little more for herself."[9] My knee-jerk reaction was, "Hey, that's me!" Since graduation from college I had been pushing myself to be the best possible wife, mother, community volunteer, church worker, teacher, friend. A few months earlier I had had the dream indicating I was to leave public school teaching. A few weeks later my co-teacher in church school pointed out the Year of Restoration, summed up in Leviticus 25:10. "In this way you shall set the fiftieth year apart and proclaim freedom to all the inhabitants of the land." Guess what year I was in? My fiftieth! So it came to pass that I did resign my job and took a year during which I relaxed into "being" more than "doing."

[8] Henri J. M. Nouwen, *The Genesee Diary: Report from a Trappist Monastery* (Garden City, N.Y.: Doubleday & Company, Inc., 1976), pp. 59, 64, 65.
[9] Gail Sheehy, *Passages: Predictable Crises of Adult Life* (New York: E. P. Dutton & Co., Inc., 1974), p. 216.

My temptation is to go running around pushing books I like into other people's hands, but I know better. Each person needs to decide for oneself *what* and *when* to read. Timing is of great consequence. An extreme case in point is the two books I have had for over thirty years that just became important to me in the last six months. So I have stopped saying, "You ought to read this book," replacing it with, "I found this book helpful. Do you want to see if it speaks to you now?" I search for my truth. You search for yours.

BEYOND WORDS

The faith of our mothers and fathers pulsates through the pages of the Bible. This best-seller continues to withstand the test of time. It has spoken, does speak, and will speak to God's people. No matter how often we turn to the same chapter, the living Word can speak a new word to us.

> The authority of the Bible is thus the authority of God who speaks through it to mankind. . . . It is required of faith that it does not deny the spirit of inquiry; and conversely it is required of the spirit of inquiry that it does not cling to prejudices as to what God can or cannot do in the sovereign activity of his word. The problem of the synthesis of faith and criticism seems to be one aspect of the larger problem of divine grace in its relation to human freedom.[10]

However glorious and inspired the words, there is a quality that transcends the medium that conveys it. We turn to the Bible, not to *know about God* but to *know God.*

"TASTE AND SEE" SUGGESTIONS
Exploratory Steps in Finding Your Way of Spiritual Growth

1. Ask yourself: What do I like about the Bible?
   What don't I like about the Bible?

2. If you live in a family situation, start reading the Bible together at least one night a week. Depending on the age of children, you may want to use a paraphrase or a book of Bible stories.

3. Consider the kind of literature that most attracts you in your usual reading and use that as a clue to a starting place in the Bible library. If you like poetry, read Psalms or the Song of Solomon. If you like drama, gather a few friends and take parts reading aloud from Job.

4. Use your imagination to flesh out some of the Bible persons. Since the writers were interested only in individuals as they contributed to God's larger purposes, the usual biographical information is missing often. For instance, did Dorcas have a family

[10]The Archbishop of Canterbury, *The Authority of the Bible, Peake's Commentary on the Bible* (Thomas Nelson and Sons Ltd., 1962), p. 7.

to rejoice with when Peter restored her life? What source of income did she have if "she spent all her time doing good and helping the poor" (Acts 9:36b, TEV)? We know Simon Peter had a mother-in-law, but what about his wife? Mark 1:29-31 infers there may have been an extended family living situation. What persons lived there and how did they relate?

5. Picture yourself in some of the teaching and/or healing episodes of Jesus as told by Matthew, Mark, or Luke. Are you up front, close to Jesus, or on the fringes of the crowd? Are you amazed? Pleased? Indifferent? Threatened? How would you report this experience at the dinner table that evening?

6. Spend some browsing time in your church library, public library, a bookstore, or perhaps by your pastor's bookshelves to see what treasures beckon to you.

7. Read *Transforming Bible Study,* by Walter Wink (Abingdon, 1980). It is a leader's guide that explains his innovative group-encounter method of approaching the Bible. It is a holistic approach, combining critical study with imagination and meditative practices. A process involving a total encounter with the Bible by all of our selves is described, including transcripts of actual group sessions.

6

Corporate Worship: Praising God Together

Praise the Lord!
Give thanks to the Lord, because he is good;
  his love is eternal.
Who can tell all the great things he has done?
Who can praise him enough?
                    —Psalm 106:1-2, TEV

When we pause to reflect on who we are: creatures made by the Creator, children cared for by the Parent, subjects of the King of Kings, moments in the Eternal, finite beings connected to the Infinite, sinners redeemed by the only Son of God, humans loved by Yahweh—there is only one appropriate response: to bow down and worship the Lord God Almighty. God's command to worship only One dovetails with our need to worship. In worship we acknowledge that God is God, and we are not.

Acknowledging and submitting to a higher power with appropriate rituals and actions is common to all cultures and all times. Paul capitalized on this evidence in Athens and declared to them the Lord of heaven and earth, who also "is actually not far from any one of us" (Acts 17:27b, TEV). Yet a submissive attitude does not always come easily to us modern achievers who have put men on the moon, erected skyscrapers, and invented a myriad labor-saving gadgets. We have also created the most monstrous weapons ever used and have abused the good earth and its resources. So pride and pretense that human efforts are sufficient crumble rather easily in me. I support all human efforts toward justice, peace, and ecology, but I know that of ourselves we can do nothing. I submit to God because *only* God can protect and comfort me.

Of course, throughout history there have been doubters, atheists, agnostics. I do not doubt their sincerity or their right to believe and act as they do. They simply are not my heroes or heroines. They did not compose Handel's *Messiah* or paint Rembrandt's *Supper at Emmaus* or, as Martin Luther King, Jr., did, nonviolently change the segregation patterns of our country. God chooses us and uses us when we grant God first place in our lives.

> Come, let us bow down and worship him;
>   let us kneel before the Lord, our Maker!
> He is our God;
>   we are the people he cares for,
>   the flock for which he provides.
> —Psalm 96:1, TEV

NEEDING A FAMILY GATHERING

God loves each one of us as an only child, yet each of us is brother or sister to everyone who claims God as Parent. Impossible, of course, except that with God all things are possible. Douglas Steere writes about the misfortune of being an only child because it precludes experiential learning that parental love is not diminished when it is shared.

> Nowhere is this psychological truth better revealed than in the relation between private and corporate worship. For central as is the relationship between the separate individual and God, each man needs an experience of life in the great family of God if he is to grow to understand the real nature of that love and the real character of his response to that love, to say nothing of growing to understand and to live creatively with his fellows.[1]

We need each other. It is too hard to be Christian alone. No way can we live out the "Good News" in today's world, be the servant-persons we are called to be, without the encouragement of frequent fellowship with other faith family members, of supporting and being supported by others who are also walking this way. Whistling alone in the dark is possible for only so long before we want to be part of a believer's chorus. The wheel analogy used by Howard Brinton reminds us that the closer we come in worship to God, the Center, the closer we, as the spokes, are to each other. Focusing on our common love of God is the firmest foundation for loving one another.

A healthy vine has not one but a profusion of shoots, as mentioned in chapter 1. Seldom are all shoots growing at the same rate. When the inevitable storms hit or the times of doubt and dryness creep in, we need not only to feel the comfort of others, but also to see all around us the evidence of healthy growth that in due season will be ours again. We are nourished first and foremost by the true Vine, but we also learn from and nurture each other.

When we participate in corporate worship we are continuing

[1]Douglas V. Steere, *Prayer and Worship* (New York: The Edward W. Hazen Foundation, Inc., 1938), pp. 36, 37.

the tradition established long ago between Yahweh and the Hebrews. Israel's ancient identity was a worshiping community ruled by the Lord. We noted in the previous chapter how biblical biographies include only the individual's contribution to the nation's welfare, since the important story was always the *group* story. Jesus followed the family sabbath custom and "went as usual to the synagogue" (Luke 4:16b, TEV). The early church "met as a group in the Temple, and they had their meals together in their homes, eating with glad and humble hearts, praising God, and enjoying the good will of all the people" (Acts 2:46-47a, TEV). Through the centuries into the present, Christians have risked persecution and death to gather together for prayer and praise. Truly we need the spiritual refreshment found in being together before the Lord.

In addition, attending public worship is a visible sign to others concerning our priorities. Perhaps God is worshiped on the golf course, but Sunday morning golfers are not generally recognized as kingdom builders, as members of the church, the Body of Christ. Putting our bodies with the Body underscores our belief that the church is necessary to us and today's world.

THE HOLY ORDINARY

In Revelation we are told about worship in heaven: "Day and night they never stop singing:

'Holy, holy, holy, is the Lord God Almighty,
  who was, who is, and who is to come.'
. . . They throw their crowns down in front of the throne and say,
'Our Lord and God! You are worthy to receive glory,
  honor, and power.
For you created all things, and by your will they were given
  existence and life.'"
—Revelation 4:8b-10b, 11 TEV

This is the same God whose only Son was born in a smelly barn, yet who sent angels to announce the event before and after. We face such incongruities and ambiguities, mysteries, and confusion, at every turn. How can we get it all together—the holiness of God and the frustrations of our daily days? We know deep down that there is a connection, but we need handles.

Regular attendance at corporate worship is one handle. The rituals, the ambience, the planned sequence of specific acts, have all been developed to foster our having a sneak preview of the glory of God and glimpsing where and how we fit in the larger scene. From his start in a stable, through his ministry with and to fishermen and other common folk, to his death between thieves, Jesus, the Son of God, lived the common life with a holy flair. In worship we pause to seek and recognize that holiness in our every-day business-as-usual lives. The holy ordinariness of life is part of worship.

The early Hebrews wrote of the *Shekinah,* the pervasive radi-ance of God. It resided in the tabernacle originally and later was understood to be personified in Christ. *Shekinah* denotes the close-ness of God, God in the midst of the gathered community, as opposed to a remote God enshrined on a distant throne. When we gather together for worship we hope to be invaded by the *Shekinah* of God.

Celebration is a dominant theme of worship. What could be more joyous than being together at our family festival honoring the One and Only? Being happy all alone is a "bummer"; happiness needs friends with whom we can share it. And when we are sad, a shoulder to cry on or at least someone with an extra tissue is certainly handy. Having a place where tears and fears and cheers are all okay is definitely something to rejoice about. Singing hymns and anthems to the Invisible Three in One may sound foolish to the worldly wise, but as Paul pointed out to the Corinthians, Christians are called to be fools in order to be truly wise. Besides, lovers often act a bit foolishly when they are together. So worship the Holy One who is in the midst of the ordinary. Celebrate with joy and abandon.

To tell you the truth—and nothing else is worth the paper, time, and effort—much of what I have written about corporate worship so far is wishful thinking. Although I have faithfully been putting *my* body with *the* Body for years, only intermittently have I broken through to the kind of worship I've been describing. Admitting this to my editor, I begged off writing about worship by reason of inadequacy, but she would have none of it. She suggested that readers may be having similar problems, so why not just deal with mine openly? I know she is right, but it does not make doing it any easier. So assuming we are in this together, let us search together for some tentative answers, or at least some possible paths to follow. The question, in case it is unclear, is: How can I connect more meaningfully through corporate worship? Or put another way, how can I experience more reality, touch Love more often, in corporate worship?

NO ONE WAY

Exodus, Leviticus, and Numbers in the Old Testament have a combined twenty-three chapters devoted to religious laws govern-ing the exact building and furnishing of a place of worship for Israel and laws regarding the priests and rituals for the worship of the Lord. In contrast, the New Testament record of the early Christian church in Acts and various letters prescribes no one pattern, but shows a variety of church forms and worship styles. Transformation, new life, beginnings are the order of the day. Traditions are being started more often than followed. Change is the significant feature of worship in the early church described in the New Testament.

At the start let us be clear that we are not looking for one ideal kind of worship service that will suit all of us. There is no such gathering, and if there were, there would be no New Testament precedent for it. Diversity in unity, rather than uniformity, is our goal. Given our human nature, diversity is inevitable. Our unity is in our common faith in Jesus Christ.

Perhaps looking at some of the different emphases found in several Christian worship traditions will be helpful. My purpose is not to judge but to note the value which is there for many worshipers, whether you or I happen to be one of them or not.

For over 1,500 years the Eastern Orthodox church has been using the same forms to make visible the covenant between God and persons. The prescribed ceremonies and dialogues combined with the architecture, art, colorful vestments and curtains, hymns and chants, incense odors, light and darkness, body postures, all contribute to the magnificent drama depicting the loving relationship between the Almighty and "the work of his hands." Alexander Schmemann, in his book aptly titled *For the Life of the World: Sacraments and Orthodoxy*,[2] emphasizes that when the church performs its liturgy it is the sacrament of the world, that is, "a visible form of invisible grace," which is St. Augustine's definition of a sacrament. The church responds in love on behalf of the whole world to the God who gave his Son to the whole world in love. The Orthodox tradition carries a clear sense of serving the world both when the church is at worship and when it is involved in mission.

The Roman Catholic church also has a long history of liturgical worship. One liturgist says, "God is in the details," and lives out his beliefs by carefully instructing participants in the meaning, timing, and enactment of each part of the liturgy. Liturgical worship services make much use of symbolic acts—procession, kneeling, lifting up the Bible, the host, and the offering—to communicate that which is beyond words. While Eucharist (thanksgiving for Christ's sacrifice) has always been the culmination of the Mass, current liturgical renewal is giving strong emphasis to the hearing of the Word. The important dates and themes of Christendom are emphasized in turn through the use of the liturgical calendar. Through seven official sacraments and many other rituals, the

---

[2] Alexander Schmemann, *For the Life of the World: Sacraments and Orthodoxy* (Crestwood, N.Y.: St. Vladimir's Seminary Press, 1973).

Roman Catholic church provides ways to mark small (a blessing of throats in February) and large (ordination, marriage) milestone events of life, ways to express the mystery and preciousness of life.

Protestant worship services vary from the formality of highly liturgical worship to the informality of a free church service which includes spontaneous testimonials. Individual congregations and their pastors develop and change worship forms according to what they feel is appropriate and helpful. The word, as read from the Bible and interpreted in the sermon, is a major focus of the worship time. A Roman Catholic friend remarked that "fellowship" is a Protestant word. This caused me to reflect on the number of small group and congregational gatherings in most Protestant churches. This frequent contact does contribute to a comfortable family closeness in many congregations during worship time. The Lord's Supper, or Communion, is experienced as communing both with God and with one another.

The Religious Society of Friends, often called Quakers, meet for worship in silence.[3] When any participant is prompted by the Spirit to share a message, he or she speaks to all. Otherwise, believers continue in a spirit of worship—listening, reflecting, and being attentive to the Inner Light. Quakers have few established rituals and none are considered sacraments. Instead, all of life is felt to be sacramental. "A sacrament is God offering his holiness to men; a ritual is men raising up the holiness of their humanity to God."[4] It can happen any time, any place.

Charismatic worship services have a minimum of form and a maximum of openness to the Holy Spirit. Following the description of Pentecost in Acts 2, charismatics value speaking in tongues, interpretative messages of the Bible, and the tongue-speaking, and songs of joyful praise. Worshipers have a willingness, even desire, to respond to the Living God in a lively way—involving their bodies and emotions as well as minds and spirits.

EFFORT AND DEPENDENCY

When the Samaritan woman raised the question of the proper place to worship, Jesus made it clear place was unimportant, and moved on to the "who" and "how" of worship. "But the time is coming and is already here, when by the power of God's Spirit, people will worship the Father as he really is, offering him the true worship that he wants. God is Spirit, and only by the power

---

[3] Silent meetings for worship which continue the early tradition of George Fox and William Penn are found mostly in the eastern United States. There are also pastoral Friends meetings with paid clergy and a traditional type of Protestant service in other parts of the U.S.

[4] Frederick Buechner, *Wishful Thinking: A Theological ABC* (New York: Harper & Row, Publishers, Inc., 1973), p. 82.

of his Spirit can people worship him as he really is" (John 4:23-24,TEV). Corporate worship is a discipline because we make the effort to gather together to be open in "holy expectancy." It is grace because we are dependent on the Spirit, God inspiring the worship God seeks.

From even our limited survey of various Christian worship forms, it is clear that congregations find many ways to praise God together and be open to the Spirit. From Jesus' words to the woman of Samaria it is also clear that forms become irrelevant when Spirit touches spirit. What is not so clear is what you and I need to do besides getting together with others at the appointed time and place. Many of us have been making that kind of effort for "lo, these many years," and are vaguely, or not so vaguely, aware that things could be better.

We could, of course, change places and worship with another congregation, which is sometimes advisable. That is, however, a very individual matter which each has to decide for himself or herself. We could try to get the minister or worship committee or elders or someone to change the worship service to our specification, but that is unfair and/or unworkable, and perhaps unhealthy—for us. So guess who is left, who needs to change? Me—and you. I am going to look at some ways I could change. You can look, too, and, as they say, if the shoe fits, put it on.

1. Consciously cultivate an attitude of "holy expectancy" through prayer. Recently I have begun praying daily and specifically for the worship leader and worshipers where I attend church. The result is, even early on, a more open attitude in me, an entering into worship with more eagerness. Years ago in a church where the feelings between pastor and people were less than cordial, a woman told me she often saw Christ in the pulpit standing by the preacher. I believe it was her deep prayer life that facilitated the vision that blessed her.

2. Participate fully in every part of the worship service. Much of the U.S. has an acute case of spectatoritis brought on by watching professionals and superstars on television. The critical mindset that this malady engenders is counterproductive to worship.

Instead of this, I need a receptiveness which is not, however, passivity. Being aware of the planned sequence in the order of worship, from praise to confession to listening to receiving to responding with gifts to a parting blessing, helps me fit into the flow. Regular attendance is an excellent habit, but stifling if I go without realizing I have a choice. Maybe it would be creative for me to be fully absent to discover I want to be fully present.

3. Let go of my requirement that every part of the worship experience suit me to a "T." I would like to remove "I didn't get

anything out of it" from my Sunday vocabulary. Instead I want to remember why I came—*to worship,* not to critique a performance. Perhaps only one line of a hymn or one phrase of a prayer or seeing sunlight through a stained-glass window or contemplating the empty cross or a lighted candle moves me deeply; but quite possibly that is enough. Maybe disconnecting from the words and just resting in the sanctuary space with its aura of peace and beauty is the best way to awaken my worshipful spirit. Sometimes the best part for me is the benediction. Don't laugh, please. It is not because it is the end, but because I so yearn for a specific spoken blessing, and my tradition provides for it in no other time or place.

4. Share more common life together. It is obvious, I guess, that the better I know others through working, studying, and praying together, the more intimate and meaningful our corporate worship time can be. Of course, closeness leads to finding out we are not all "Goody Two Shoes." Differences discovered sometimes lead to friction producing more heat than light. Regardless of the time and pain involved, I want to risk more "speaking the truth in love" and forgiving "seventy times seven," especially within the church family. It is easy to understand why the New Testament letters to the new churches contain so many practical comments about relating to each other.

5. Value all worship traditions. I grew up in a time when Catholics and Protestants mixed about as well as oil and water, but Vatican II sent fresh breezes which are blowing away my provincial Protestant attitude. I don't have to become a Roman Catholic to benefit from remembering the liturgical year, or a Quaker to consider all of life sacramental. I need only to be open to truth and light wherever I find them. What music to my ears when a Roman Catholic friend responded to my statement about our different traditions, "But your church *is* my church—the Christian church." There is great freedom in not having to defend my worship style as *the* way.

SMALL IS BEAUTIFUL

We don't need a crowd or a formal church service to engage in corporate worship. "Where two or three are gathered in my name, there am I in the midst of them," may be over-quoted but it cannot be over-lived. The Presence is available, and from Presence issues power.

Small groups that meet for Bible study and/or prayer and/or mission and/or support may casually or purposefully include worship in their together time. Deep personal sharing and exploring of our feelings usually do not happen in large groups. We need a small intimate setting to facilitate sharing and trust building. The more intimately we know God and ourselves, the more we know God is Love and the more we want to worship the God of Love. Small gatherings provide safe places to experiment with adapting old forms or creating new ones. A silent pruning and arranging of early spring flowering branches was a powerful sermon for one small worshiping community.

If we feel a need, there is nothing to stop us from having midweek gatherings for worship in our homes. Each person can claim his or her priesthood. We can continually challenge and support one another in finding our gifts to be used within the group for the enrichment of all. Every one of us can be a "priest" to others within a limited defined area. Or maybe it is better said: All acknowledge God as Gift-Giver and each of us as a gifted person shares responsibility for the group life with mutual accountability.

When we come together to give and receive ministry and to share our hurts and joys, a community develops that is bound by more than human closeness. In one such lay group I was surprised to hear that the one preaching did not always communicate with the one planning the rest of the service. Usually there was a discernible continuity anyway, but if not, they believed that they met the various needs of the worshipers better by following their individual leadings.

A family is a natural small group setting for intimate worship experiences. One of my biggest "if only"s is: if only I had known how or risked more or made time for more family celebrations and/or worship when my children were young. As Sam Mackintosh says, "whatever helps the kids to grow 'in wisdom, age, and grace,' whatever promotes their natural sense of awe in the face of the universe, whatever increases their delight in the world, is 'religious.'" Family worship is not always a matter of a special ceremony, but can be an attitude which lifts the ordinary out of "just the ordinary." I remember a one-inch tall bean sprout arching out of a paper cup that was the centerpiece on the family dinner table. Although the kindergarten gardener was the fifth child of a busy working mother, her mother had neatly lettered a card, "Behold, Chrissie's bean!" and given it a special prominence. I believe that the mother's use of a biblical word (behold) and placement of the item on the communal dining table was a powerful if subtle message for Chrissie. A reservoir of similar experiences gathered over the years of family living is bound to enhance Chrissie's more formal worship experiences. And the adults who are privileged to share in these experiences are brought closer to "the little child" who leads.

The Hebrew sabbath and holy days are still beautifully celebrated in Jewish homes today as they had been a thousand years

before Christ. In my opinion Christians made a big mistake when
they moved out of the synagogue without taking along family
worship rituals. Of course, there is nothing to keep us from rec-
tifying the mistake, even at this late date, and adding a few more
holy days.

> Organizing an autumn moon-viewing party, baking ladders of bread
> for Rosh Hoshanna, making a cross of glory from yellow and gold
> marigolds on September 14, feast day of the Holy Cross, making a
> 'hut' or 'booth' of cornstalks and autumn leaves for Succoth—all of
> these things are ways of being co-creators along with God, of giving
> birth to the new creation, of making beauty (the glory of God: DOXA),
> of helping our children to see that they are indeed kings/queens/
> priests of creation, truly Royal Persons. . . . But so much works against
> us in our culture, not excluding much in the Church itself . . . . a wise
> man has said, 'the great task of our time is the restoration of the
> symbolic life.'[5]

Probably the biggest challenge is that of creating meaningful
new rituals to connect with our modern mechanized life-style. The
most glaring omission, in my mind, is the absence of a way to
sanctify the responsibility concurrent with receiving a driver's
license at age sixteen. How much we need a blessing to match the
horsepower privileges conveyed by that small card! Worship is a
conscious relating of the common experiences of life to God, the
Ultimate, and what is more common than driving a car in today's
world? Appendix C contains some helpful information on liturgy,
rituals, celebrations, and symbols.

I know I have not provided THE answer to: How can I experience
more reality, touch Love more often, in corporate worship? But I
hope you have found some clues or stimulation to continue your
individual search.

THE OTHER PART

Praising God together is only one part of our worship of the
Almighty who pitched a tent among us, as a newcomer to a Friends
silent meeting for worship found out. After minutes and minutes
of "nothing happening" he asked, "When does the service begin?"
The response was, "When the meeting ends."

"TASTE AND SEE" SUGGESTIONS
Exploratory Steps in Finding Your Way of Spiritual Growth

1. Be more intentional about observing Habakkuk 2:20 when

[5]Sam Mackintosh, *Greenblade*, September, 1980, pp. 10-11. *Greenblade*
began as a homespun mimeographed newsletter. In August, 1981, it appeared
under the title *Family Festivals* for the first time. *Family Festivals* is published
by Resource Publications, Box 444, Saratoga, CA 95070. Sam continues as
editor.

you enter the sanctuary: "The Lord is in his holy Temple; let everyone on earth be silent in his presence."

2. Practice arriving at Sunday worship ten minutes early to engage in:

Adoring, contemplating the majesty of God,

Lifting the leaders of worship into the Light of Christ,

Interceding in prayer for another worshiper(s).

3. Reflect on numbers and worship and you. Do you prefer to worship "where two or three are gathered" or with one hundred or one thousand? Or does it matter?

4. List all the types of corporate worship services you have attended. What common elements do you discern?

5. Decide what you would change if you could change *one* thing about you and corporate worship. What is your next step in facilitating that?

6. Suggest to your minister that she/he print the Bible texts used in the worship service in advance so members of the congregation may read and pray about them the preceding week.

7. An article by Charles M. Olsen says, "People, I discover, bring needs to express in worship and prayer which are impossible for the corporate sanctuary service to satisfy. We have promised more through the 'go to church' admonition than we can deliver."[6] He believes we each need "closet time" (private prayer time), "house time" (a small group), and "sanctuary time" (corporate worship). Are you giving yourself all three?

[6] Charles M. Olsen, "The Closet, the House and the Sanctuary," *The Christian Century*, December 9, 1981.

7

Growing New Branches: Beginning Steps

If you have read this far, you have a desire to grow spiritually but may be uncertain about what to do next. Many practices have been described and you probably have responded to different ones with varying degrees of enthusiasm: "I do that" . . . "That sounds really strange" . . . "Hm-m-m, that's interesting" . . . "I don't think I'm ready for that" . . . "I tried that once, but couldn't stay with it". . . .

Wherever you are, however you feel, whatever you do or don't do presently in keeping Christian spiritual disciplines, know that God loves and accepts you as you are, just because you are you. BUT also know that God wishes further to bless, love, and empower you, AND it is the nature of living things to grow. "Remain in the vine" clearly infers that we be *growing branches,* not dead wood. The writer recognized the importance of growth when he said, "Son, when you stop learning, you will soon neglect what you already know" (Proverbs 19:27, TEV). Having a sincere desire to know God is a necessary prerequisite, but it is not enough. We must establish personal priorities, develop new habits.

DAILY TIME WITH GOD

Giving top priority to God—keeping the first commandment— *by setting aside time each day for prayer and Bible use* is basic. Taking time every day is a discipline (noun)—"training which corrects, molds, strengthens or perfects" [Webster]. It requires discipline (verb)—"to train in self-control or obedience to given standards" [Webster]. "Discipline" and "disciple" both come from the same root word which indicates that we cannot be true disciples without discipline.

Discipline does not have an inviting connotation for most of us. Yet this stumbling block called discipline, which we procrastinate about adopting, is the cornerstone of a committed Christian life-style. Taking time each day is the hard part, the discipline, at

least until our quiet time with God becomes a daily routine, and/
or so rewarding that we eagerly anticipate it.

However, our time with God need not, should not, ever become
only routine or dull routine. While some form of prayer and Bible
use (the subjects of chapters 2, 3, and 4 are all prayer forms) are
needed every day by Christians, the Infinite God who has created
each of us as a unique individual encourages us to follow our
preferences, listen to our inner leadings. Having resolved to spend
time daily with God, most of us will benefit by starting with what
is most appealing and easy, and gradually experimenting with
other spiritual practices as our need and opportunities direct. The
challenge is to keep growing.

Many people find early morning the best time. I finally realized
why when I reflected on my own list-making habit. Although I
make numerous and long lists, I seldom get everything crossed off
a particular list. I usually do the first item and sometimes the
second and third. After that things don't get done—there are
interruptions, mood changes, and so on. What we do first, we do.
It's as simple as that. One woman went about in a euphoric state
for a week because she was so pleased with her decision to begin
keeping disciplines. She was going to take some quiet time as soon
as she did the dishes . . . started the laundry . . . made a phone
call. . . . Finally she realized it takes more than a mental decision.
It takes *doing*. Ben Franklin noted our human frailty some years
ago: "Well done is better than well said," and "How many observe
Christ's Birthday; How few his Precepts! O! 'tis easier to keep
Holidays than Commandments."[1]

Whether our time turns out to be morning, noon, or night, each
of us needs to carve out a special private quiet time and place to
be alone with ourselves and our God. Keep experimenting until
you find the right time for you. You deserve it, and God is worth
it. A few real life stories may provide some usable clues.

Age and stage of life make a difference. I confess I am not a
morning person. For years I thought the hardest thing I did each
day was getting out of bed. Then, at age 49, I attended a weekend
mini-experience of the "Journey Inward, Journey Outward"[2] spon-
sored by the Wellspring mission group of The Church of the Saviour, Washington, D.C. It was good news! I knew I wanted the
power and direction in my life that I saw in those committed
Christians. I came home, set the alarm one-half hour early, and
got up. And wonder of wonders, I continued! My lack of verbal
communication skills at that early hour was an advantage when

[1] Ben Franklin, *Ben Franklin's Wit & Wisdom* (Mount Vernon, N.Y.: Peter
Pauper Press), pp. 7, 12.

[2] Elizabeth O'Connor, *Journey Inward, Journey Outward* (New York: Harper
& Row, Publishers, Inc., 1968).

meeting with God instead of the disadvantage it was when coping with the family at breakfast. So cheer up, all you grouchy-in-the-morning persons. God accepts all who come, in any mood, with any disposition.

An insomniac I knew considered her sleeplessness an opportunity for intercessory prayer. "I often wake up at 4 A.M.," she said, "and reach for my prayer list." She belonged to a prayer group that circulated typed lists of people's specific needs and rejoiced in this way to help because her health prevented active physical work.

A man who is away from home eleven hours a day working in the corporate world regularly listens to symphonic music in the evening. He has unsuccessfully tried silent meditation, imaging, and keeping a journal. Obviously his spirit is renewed, his soul refreshed, but he can find no words to express what happens. Yet he knows that music meets his need. Although this is not generally considered a classic Christian discipline, Helen M. Luke considers music "the highest spiritual experience.[3] Many of us could use a David with harp to soothe our frenzied Saul self.

As a child, total incredulity was my reaction to overhearing an adult church school teacher say she spent one hour each morning on Bible study preparing for her class. I thought Saturday, or even Saturday night, was made for getting ready for Sunday. Yet her practice no longer sounds strange, but rather sensible. Bible study and devotional Bible reading are quite compatible. At the very least, Bible knowledge is an easily retrieved resource to be reflected on and/or applied in moments of routine physical work, commuting, whatever.

My friend says Protestants learn their theology through their hymns. I like to keep our church bulletins that contain the words of hymns in my car; when I drive alone I have a great time singing. David was alone on a hillside with his sheep when he composed psalms. I'm alone in my car on a busy highway, especially in winter when I have the windows closed.

For some persons it is easier to block out an entire weekend than to find bits and pieces of time in their daily routine. A silent retreat, an inspiring conference or a camping weekend with a few like-minded, seeking friends may be the ideal launching event for some.

These are just examples of beginning steps. You must decide what is possible for you and begin there. As the saying goes, "The longest journey begins with but a single step." Chances are that even beginning with a small step, you will have

---

[3]Helen M. Luke, *Woman, Earth and Spirit: The Feminine in Symbol and Myth* (New York: The Crossroad Publishing Company, 1981), p. 22.

lapses. Don't waste energy hanging onto guilt. Try again. I live near a two-year residential drug rehabilitation home named "Gaudenzia House." It is named for a horse that competed in a long steeplechase in France. Gaudenzia fell several times during the race but always got up and ran on, eventually winning the event. When you stumble, shout, "Hi, ho, Gaudenzia," and get back on your chosen path.

A CARING CHECKER

In addition to being intentional about our spiritual growth by having a definite time, place, and practice to be aware of God's presence, we need a structure of accountability. While it is not impossible to keep Christian spiritual disciplines on our own, it is very difficult without someone to check regularly that we are actually doing what we have said we want to do. We are fallible beings; Paul knowingly speaks of the human condition when he says, "I do not understand what I do; for I don't do what I would like to do, but instead I do what I hate" (Romans 7:15, TEV). We need another person who cares enough to ask, "How are you?" and then listens with acceptance when we dare answer how it really is with us. At times we also need someone to answer our "What do I do in my quiet time?" and "How am I doing?"

A spiritual director is a person who provides this care. He or she is a co-pilgrim who walks with another and is an instrument of God's love and guidance in that person's life. Spiritual direction involves a concern for the whole person—physically, psychologically, and spiritually—as she or he responds to God's call to discipleship. The roots of this tradition stretch back into the early church and through the centuries of Christendom. Although it has never been widely practiced, a faithful remnant has preserved it. Catholic orders have prescribed ways of spiritual formation. Individual Christians have sought and found one or a few like-motivated persons to encourage and share with in depth. Spiritual direction has been largely an oral tradition practiced as a one-to-one intimate, trusted relationship.

However, for three years I enjoyed spiritual direction by mail, plus one or two retreats or workshops annually, all through the Wellspring mission group. I summarized my inner and outer journey every two weeks on the left half of a page and my spiritual director responded on the right half of the paper. (The outline for this is given in Appendix D.) Almost everyone to whom I mention this objects initially with, "That sounds like having to do a report for school. I'm not sure I like that." For me it was a tremendously affirming, growth-producing experience. Often I could write more honestly and in greater depth than I could have spoken face to face. There was no grade-giving teacher on the other end. There was an understanding, accepting, encouraging, more experienced pilgrim. Lapses were met not with reprimands or put-downs, but caring questions such as "What is blocking you?" and "Why do you think it is so hard to find time?" Now I meet every three weeks with a Catholic nun who lives in my area. She has a very busy schedule and can't accept a written responsibility, but I still make my own written summary to help keep my loose tongue and my detour-prone mind on target. I am also blessed with uncommonly close and caring friends. My time alone with God is essential. So are accountability, physical hugs, and honest human feedback.

> A faithful friend is a sure shelter,
>   whoever finds one has found a rare treasure.
> A faithful friend is something beyond price,
>   there is no measuring his worth.
> A faithful friend is the elixir of life,
>   and those who fear the Lord will find one.
> Whoever fears the Lord makes true friends,
>   for as a man is, so is his friend.
>   —Ecclesiasticus 6:14-17, Jerusalem

This special friendship of support and guidance that one Christian can give another is described in several recent books with illustrative titles: *Spiritual Friend, Soul Friend,* and *Faithful Friendship.*[4] Their appearance, among others, indicates the current need and interest Christians are feeling for help in spiritual growth. The Shalem Institute for Spiritual Formation in Washington, D.C., and the Guild for Spiritual Direction at Wainwright House in Rye, New York, offer two-year night and/or weekend programs to develop the gifts of persons called to spiritual direction. Finding a spiritual advisor with special training and experience would undoubtedly be a great blessing, but it is not the only route. Dorothy C. Devers's *Faithful Friendship* is written specifically for use by two Christians who wish to be mutually accountable. She even counsels that a spiritual director need not take herself or himself too seriously. If God is taken seriously, God will get the work done.

COME AS A CHILD

In addition to keeping faithfully a special time with God and finding a caring checker (spiritual guide), a childlike attitude is necessary. Jesus said, ". . . I assure you that whoever does not receive the Kingdom of God like a child will never enter it" (Mark

[4]Tilden H. Edwards, *Spiritual Friend* (New York: Paulist Press, 1980). Kenneth Leech, *Soul Friend* (London: Sheldon Press, 1977). Dorothy C. Devers, *Faithful Friendship;* this book is privately printed and available from Potter's House Book Service, 1658 Columbia Road, N.W., Washington, DC 20009.

10:15, TEV). When born into a loving family, children's openness
to life is coupled with a certainty that parents will take care of
them, come what may. Movement toward this childlike faith—
both toward new ways of experiencing God in our private time
and toward changes in our life that we may be called to—is our
task. Let us explore some childlike traits that can enhance our
spiritual growth.

*Curiosity, taking risks, trying new things, stepping out into the
unknown* are all part of childhood. When we have little or no
remembered past, there is nothing to do but step out into the
future. As we grow older, instead of allowing God to temper us
with the fires of hurtful experience, we sometimes decide to avoid
all fires (play it safe) and so become cold and rigid. As New Testament persons we must remember that on Pentecost the Holy
Spirit came as fire! Fire is exciting, scary, and dangerous. Children
like to play with fire, literally and figuratively. Without throwing
caution completely to the winds, can we risk more new adventures?

After my years of focusing on areas where I could make A's, or
better yet A +, my first spiritual director wrote, "Know that you
will make mistakes." What new advice! She invited me to accept
the freedom to fail—a concept which somehow had completely
eluded me despite all the church's talk about our being sinners.
Hearing that good news was a turning point for me. I began to
change old patterns, risk new behavior. The child who could see
with fresh eyes and explore new ways was reborn.

The Bible is about newness from creation in Genesis to a new
heaven and a new earth in Revelation. God is Lord of the future
as Isaiah reveals (Isaiah 48:6b-7a). Paul's word about the need for
constant renewal is as applicable to our church as to the believers
at Colossae (Colossians 3:9-10). Jesus spoke continually of new
things—new fabric, new wine, new growth from seeds—and acted
in new ways—forgiving enemies, washing feet, and finally dying
for the unworthy. Possibly the most disturbing observation about
Christianity is not that it has failed, but that it has not been tried
enough. Look for the new thing God is calling you to.

Play, stories, imagination make up a large part of a child's world.
Children feel a freedom to be anyone, with or without costumes
and props. Such imaginative openness is a wonderful talent to
bring to the Bible. Take a turn being each character in a story or
parable. How do you feel? What posture is appropriate? What tone
of voice do you use? Why are you acting this way? Fill in missing
details and background of the story as you wish. Even try several
different possibilities. "Living into" a scene this way can bring a
vitality that ordinary reading seldom does. The same method can
be helpful when dealing prayerfully with an unsatisfactory rela-

tionship. With absolute honesty, even ruthlessness, say (shout?) all you feel and think to the other (imagined) person. Then be that person and repeat the process. After exposing and experiencing both sides through *imagination,* we have a greater freedom to decide what we *actually* want to say and do.

I have never met a child who would not sit still to listen to a good story. A good storyteller does not moralize. She or he simply tells the story and lets the "a-ha!" come or not, as it will. We in Western civilization are heirs of two types of knowing: the Greek way to truth via logic and the Hebrew way to truth via story. Our culture strongly emphasizes the Greek way and its outgrowth— the scientific rational approach. The Bible, of course, is written in the Hebrew tradition which says history has a story to tell and the main actor is God. God also speaks through nature—"The heavens tell out the glory of God" (Psalm 19:1a, NEB)—and through persons—prophets, priests, you, and me. We, too, can come as children to sit and listen. Come listen to nature, in a running brook, a starry sky, a budding rose, a wobbly foal. Come listen to each other's stories. Come listen to the stories of the Bible.

Children's imagination is often delightful. Our third son had an imaginary green dog for some months. We laughed, of course, but it obviously met his need for a "man's best friend" that his parents were unwilling to provide immediately. His choice of color fills me with wonder. Green is the color of the Holy Spirit—according to Carl Jung, because of its spermatic, procreative quality. If you can't love someone, imagine Jesus hugging that person. Bring Christ in imagination to any need, any situation.

While still a child Elizabeth Gray Vining discovered that imagination is stronger than willpower. She had to pass a candy store on her way home from school. If she pictured herself walking quickly by the store as she left school, she was able actually to do so at the crucial moment. If she allowed herself a mental image of herself in the shop with the goodies, she went in despite an earlier determination not to do so. She adds, "Similarly I learned that if I pictured myself approaching my homework with total concentration, I could work away at it oblivious to distractions and finish it in half the time."[5]

To create, to make a new thing, we first must image it. "So God created man in his own image . . . male and female he created them" (Genesis 1:27, NEB). Children create images using crayons, paint, sand, clay (or mud), paper, junk, etc. Using any of these media to create a new thing can put us in touch with hidden parts

[5] Elizabeth Gray Vining, *Harnessing Pegasus,* Pendle Hill Pamphlet 221 (Lebanon, Pa.: Sowers Printing Company, 1978), p. 5.

of ourselves—and can therefore be a growth experience. Imagination is a valuable resource for all ages. It's fun and it works!

Children are needy. They can't provide for themselves. They are dependent on others to nurture their bodies, minds, and spirits. From their earliest cries through their "gimme's" to the "I need the car tonight," they are quite forthright about stating their desires. In many ways Jesus made it clear that he came to sinners, to the wounded, to the needy. The first beatitude has been paraphrased: Blessed are those who by the Spirit know they are in need of God.

I have learned the importance of listening to my deepest desires, my real needs. After looking at all facets of a situation I often ask myself, "What do I really *want* to do?" I trust the answering inner pull toward a particular action. It has taken me to the bedside of an injured friend in another state at just the right time. Yesterday it caused me to stop writing (despite the publisher's deadline) to bake cookies to share. I often use this question in my daily hour with God to discern which Bible use and prayer forms I most need. Having established and confessed my basic need of God, following my deep wants and needs proves 90 percent of the time to be what God wants for me. Truly, God is found in the heart of a needy child. Look within—to your needs and to God.

REJOICE—YOU'RE DIFFERENT!

The basics—being disciplined about time with God, acquiring a spiritual guide and accountability structure, and becoming childlike before God—are not equally easy for individuals to carry out. We have differing gifts, differing aptitudes—not higher and lower, better and worse—just different. All of the disciplines are means, not ends. The only purpose of the disciplines is to put us in the place to receive God's love and grace. Any discipline that puts *you* in the right place for that to happen is the right one for you.

A practical realist will probably value corporate worship over private prayer and will be interested in the way the service is conducted. A more introverted person will appreciate religious externals as symbols, as pointers to the unseen world. Artistic persons enjoy using their imagination with Bible stories and connect easily with drama, dance, and art. A "thinker" may write out his or her own prayers systematically, relating personal faith to the world we live in, and then use them in private devotional times. Others who are more aware of their feelings may pray spontaneously expressing gratitude, fear, trust, love, anger, penitence. Journal writing is a tremendous release for some, while others see only a threatening white page. Go with what feels right and good to you.

This business of valuing differences is easier said than done.

There is a Henry Higgins in all of us, I suspect, wondering why a woman can't be more like a man—or, more broadly, why *you* aren't more like *me*. Living out Jesus' second commandment— loving others and myself—has been much easier since I discovered the Myers-Briggs Type Indicator, a psychological tool that identifies and describes sixteen different types of people. It provides the most helpful handle I know for identifying and enjoying differences. My marriage, my friendships, and even my dealings with my "enemies," have benefited from my understanding of types. Paul's writings about gifts—Romans 12 and 1 Corinthians 12— have likewise been greatly enhanced and clarified.

When I observe the multitudinous variety in the plant world, the amazing diversity in the animal kingdom, and the astounding differences of color, size, and shape among our human family, I can only conclude that our Creator enjoys uniqueness. So might we! Especially our own. Your relationship with God is unique; your process of becoming who you really are is unique; your empowerment to act in the world is unique. You are the only valid authority for you. Therefore, choose from these pages what "speaks" to you. Trust the Spirit to guide you to what you need. Trust yourself, for at your deepest level is the image of God within. Rejoice in your uniqueness.

CHANGES

I have been serious about keeping Christian spiritual disciplines for almost six years, and there are some observable changes in me. I am much more aware that life is a series of death and resurrection experiences. As I risk letting go of an old self so it can die, a new one is born. The process is neither easy nor painless, but it is definitely rewarding. Once after going through a difficult struggle, I asked my spiritual director if the next one would be any easier. She replied, "No, but it will be different." She was right.

Some of the changes I have noticed in myself are:

I am more willing to volunteer where I feel "called,"
 and less influenced by nominating committees.
I am more ready to share my gifts,
 and less responsive to, "We need somebody to. . . ."
I am more willing to try new things, start groups, risk failure,
 and less reluctant to resign and/or end my involvement in
 groups.
I am more attentive to the breath of the Holy Spirit,
 and less subject to the winds of chance and culture.
I am more glad to be alive, whether I'm up or down,
 and less critical of moods in myself and others.

I am more aware of and dependent on God's love and grace,
and less able to claim any merit of my own.

I know myself, my many selves, better. I realize that my life
rhythm is one of intense activity followed by a resting period.
Sometimes I am visibly involved in my local church—in teaching,
resettling a refugee family, or leading a small group. At other
times I have a very low profile in my local church as I serve in
quiet ways, relating personally one-to-one, doing what I term my
"individual ministries." Recognizing my own pattern and feeling
comfortable about it is a freeing thing. When I am free to be me,
I want you to be you. I let go of my need to control others. I like
myself better and so do my family and friends.

Spirituality is living life with Spirit added. My inward journey
leads me to my outward journey. My outward journey depends on
my inward one. On both journeys I remember and am glad: We
are called to be faithful, not successful.

To bear much fruit, we must remain in the Vine. Begin where
you are. Keep a daily time with the Vinedresser. Find an accountability structure—a spiritual director, a faithful friend, or a small
group. Start with the discipline(s) that is most natural and comfortable to you, but keep growing—trying different ways, stretching out in new directions. Know that you will make mistakes; you
are human. Value your uniqueness. Be who you really are: God's
precious child.

"TASTE AND SEE" SUGGESTIONS
Exploratory Steps in Finding Your Way of Spiritual Growth

1. Read of different ways Jesus responded to persons. With
which do you most identify?
Luke 5:12-15—healing a man with skin disease
Matthew 8:18-22—would-be followers
Matthew 9:18-26—healing a child, a woman
Luke 10:25-30—giving rest
Mark 9:14-29—healing by prayer
2. Sing some of your favorite hymns or songs of any kind. Think
about the words. Do they express your beliefs?
3. What do you like about having a "faithful friend" or "spiritual
director"? What don't you like about it? Have you had any relationship similar to this to date?
4. Remember the times (if any) when you have been aware of
God's presence. Were they on a mountaintop, in a church, at a
birth or death, by the ocean, at a conference . . . ?
5. Mull over the possibilities of rearranging your home and job
routines to reduce stress and hurry in order to create more quiet
and relaxation.

6. Learn more about what types you and others close to you are according to Jungian typology. Contact a psychologist or other qualified person about taking a Myers-Briggs Type Indicator or read *Please Understand Me: An Essay on Temperament Styles* by David Keirsey and Marilyn Bates (Del Mar, California: Promethean Books, Inc., 1978).

7. Invite yourself to a mini-experience of what Elizabeth O'Connor describes in her book *Journey Inward, Journey Outward*. Three-day workshops are available in various parts of the country. Write for information to: Wellspring, 11301 Neelsville Church Road, Germantown, MD 20767.

Appendix A

Guidelines for Making Your Own Meditation Tape

Slowly read the following to make your own tape: "As a deer longs for a stream of cool water, so I long for you, O God, I thirst for you, the living God. Grant me your grace as I prepare my body, mind, and spirit to meet you.

"Lie flat on your back on the floor on a rug or blanket. Close your eyes. Spread your feet apart a little bit. Let your toes fall outward. Rest your arms on the floor at a forty-five degree angle to your body, palms up. Relax the small of your back into the rug. Free every part of your body as much as possible from all tension. Take slow deep breaths, beginning each one with the lower abdomen filling out like a balloon. *One,* inhale (wait three seconds), exhale (wait three seconds). Continue counting in this fashion through eight.

"Slowly bring your legs together. Spread your arms out to a ninety degree position. Slowly raise your right leg. Keeping your right shoulder and arm on the floor, let your straight right leg fall across your body and toward the floor leftwards. Return to the original position. Repeat the same stretch with your left leg. Take a deep breath and slowly sit up.

"Bend your left leg keeping it on the floor, left foot against right thigh. Keep your right leg straight in front of you touching the floor. Take a deep breath while raising your arms straight above your head, with thumbs hooked together. Exhale and bend forward from the waist, grabbing your right shin, ankle, toes, or whatever you can reach. Keeping the right knee unbent, relax a bit more with each out-breath. Gently move your fingers up your leg, giving yourself a mini massage. Relax your hands in your lap. Take a deep breath and repeat on left leg. Take another deep breath.

"Next, a rocking motion. Sit cross-legged, keeping your legs close to your body. Grasp one foot in each hand around the toes. Let your chin fall on your chest as you rock backward and forward three or four times, gaining momentum until your feet touch (or almost) the floor behind your head. Unwind and take a deep breath.

"This is called 'pose of the child.' Remember Samuel, who was taught by Eli to respond, 'Speak, Lord, your servant is listening.' Get in a kneeling position, sit back on your legs. Bend forward from the waist until your forehead touches the floor. Rest your arms close to your body with palms up, hands by your feet. Hold this position several minutes or as long as is comfortable.

"Again lie on your back, and count eight slow deep breaths as before.

"Relax your whole body, part by part, by tensing and relaxing it. Tense your toes. Relax. Tense your legs. (Point your heels, not toes, to prevent cramps.) Relax. Repeat for buttocks, chest, hands, arms, shoulders, neck, jaw, eyes, total body. Let go. Let go. Let go. Thank you, Lord, for the gift of your Holy Spirit which is available to me." (Now tape five or ten minutes of silence) "Thank you, Father.* Thank you, Jesus. Thank you, Holy Spirit. Amen. Amen. Amen."

*A word about using "Father." I consider myself a Christian feminist. However, language used in prayer is a very personal thing. Very early in life, before specific memory, I picked up the idea that we all have two fathers, an earthly and a heavenly one. My own father had his limitations (like all humans) and I liked having an additional One. I also, at times, refer to God as She. I long for the day when we all have and give each other permission to address our God with whatever word is right for us, even if this sounds strange in unison. Imagine what Pentecost sounded like!

Appendix B

Dreams as Symbolic Language

We all dream every night. Scientific research confirms that. Still many people say they don't dream. Others more accurately report that they don't remember their dreams. Anyone with an open, scientific attitude who wishes to test the hypothesis that we do dream and can remember our dreams can do so any night. The lab is your bedroom. The research instruments are a flashlight, paper, and pencil. The method is to promise yourself confidently upon retiring that you will wake up and write down your dream(s). It works. The images are there. We need only to value them enough to welcome and record them. Prompt recording is important because otherwise most of our dreams are lost to us.

The Bible is full of dreamers, dreams, and visions—Jacob's ladder dream, Daniel, Ezekiel, Jesus' earthly father, Paul, John's visions in Revelation, to name a few. The church in our time has been mostly silent about this important segment of Scripture. Morton Kelsey's research shows that for fifteen centuries Christians accepted dreams as a natural way for God to break into our lives. For me, as for biblical persons, dreams are evidence of a God who cares enough to send me personal messages. I don't believe I would be writing this book if I had not started paying attention to my dreams five years ago and followed the guidance I found there.

Interpreting dreams seems to be much easier for some than others. Joseph, son of Jacob, was obviously gifted in this area. His gift got him into trouble with his brothers but later paved his way to high office with the Pharaoh. *It is crucial to know that dreams are symbolic language.* An initial reaction to this is often: Why does God send me a message in a code I don't know? Probably because symbols carry emotion better than ideas or words, which is also why we use symbols in our places of worship. I find the stronger the feeling level of my dream, the more important the message for my life. Reflection, praying for guidance, and telling a trusted friend your dream are all helpful beginning steps in understanding your dreams. Reading just a few books[1] was enough to open up a wide, wonderful window toward God for me.

There are several kinds of dreams, but a very common one seems to be the compensatory dream, one that shows us a side of ourselves we are not recognizing in our conscious lives. For example, a woman feeling incompetent and lacking self-esteem dreams she is in high school receiving an award for all-around excellence. Or a man who considers himself very kind, moral, and polite dreams of a tyrannical prison guard. When we dream of other people, the message is rarely about that person. Instead, that person is a stand-in for one of our selves, one facet of our personality. Since dreams are very personal, it is my impression of that person that matters. If I dream of Sue, my very efficient friend, the message may be that I need to stop wasting time and get busy. If I dream of Hank, whom I consider rather loose with the truth, I need to discover where I am being less than honest with myself. By sending us dreams God does not force us to change, or even listen, but as always offers a message.

[1] A few of my favorite books about dreams are:

John A. Sanford, *Dreams: God's Forgotten Language* (New York: J. B. Lippincott Company, 1968).

Morton Kelsey, *Dreams, A Way to Listen to God* (New York: Paulist Press, 1978).

C. G. Jung, *Memories, Dreams, Reflections* (New York: Vintage Books, 1965).

Appendix C

Guidelines About Rituals, Symbols, and Liturgy

From the initiation rites of neolithic times to modern presidential inaugurations and blowing out candles on your birthday cake, rituals and customs have played an important role in the life of all. Following are a few words of explanation and comment about each of these crucial human activities.

LITURGY

"Liturgy" is a Greek word meaning "public work" or "the work of the people." In Greek times, if a rich citizen did something for the public—had a road built, set up a monument, made a public park—his work was called a *liturgios*. Later Christians used the word for the public service they rendered to others by their prayer in common, especially by the eucharist. Eventually the word came to mean any religious service involving ritual and ceremony; even Jews now speak of the "liturgy of the synagogue."

The best definition I know of liturgy is: "what happens when people of the biblical tradition come together to pray." That understanding covers everything from a mass said by a pope with thousands participating, to the monthly "Lord's Supper" at the local Presbyterian church, and to two or three Quakers sitting together in silence "waiting on the Lord." What I like best about the word "liturgy" is the implication that when it happens the whole world is better off. We who are rich in the things of the Spirit do our public work for others; as Byzantine Christians say, we do it "on behalf of all, and for all."

CUSTOMS AND TRADITIONS

A custom is *anything* we do or say on a given occasion. If, when someone sneezes, you usually say, "God bless you," that's a custom. If your family always has spaghetti for Thursday night supper, that's a custom. If Uncle Joe always sends a check for one hundred dollars to the parents of a new baby in the family, that's a custom. It's obvious that customs may or may not be religious.

105

Traditions are simply "corporate customs": the customs of an extended family, of a local Masonic lodge, of an ethnic group, or of any group. Americans traditionally have turkey on Thanksgiving Day; Scottish people have *haggis* (sheep's stomach) on January 25. If, when Uncle Joe died, members of the family decided to continue his custom of sending one hundred dollars to parents of newborns, that could become a family tradition. Traditions and customs aren't difficult to understand; they are what individuals and groups "always" do on specific occasions.

RITUALS AND SYMBOLS

Rituals and symbols are a bit more difficult to talk about, for two reasons: "ritual" nowadays has negative connotations; "ritualistic" means "something done compulsively, without much attention to the meaning." (Precisely the opposite of what a ritual really is!) And the word "symbol" has been so misused, especially in church circles, that misconceptions are hard to overcome. I'll start with symbols; more accurately, I'll start with what symbols are *not*.

Symbols are not "things that stand for other things." For example, the letters "XP" on an altar covering are *not* "a symbol for Christ." Nor is an egg "a symbol of the resurrection," nor a dove "the symbol of peace." Talking about symbols in that way does nothing for anyone. The only kind of response you'll get if you tell someone "a circle is the symbol for eternity" is—at best—a shrug.

Symbols are not about abstractions like "eternity" or "peace," nor are they mere decorations added on to other things. Most importantly, symbols are *not explainable*. The more rationally clear a "symbol" is, the less it really is a symbol. If you can explain a symbol—tell what it "means"—then you've killed it. The life is gone; its power lost.

SYMBOLS. A symbol is precisely an attempt to express something that can *not* be put into words. It is the best we can do—using color, fabric, signs, gestures, etc.—to express what is in our hearts but which we are unable to express verbally. (*Not,* please note, because we don't know what we want to say, but rather because of the richness and fullness of what is in our hearts.) Whether it is a kiss, a handshake, a deep bow, shared food, a beautiful piece of fabric, or whatever, a symbol is always an attempt to express something beyond words, something important— something that matters to us immensely—but which we· cannot put into words. For this reason, all symbols are religious, in that they are always expressions of what is important to us, of what really *matters to us*.

RITUAL. The difference between ritual and symbol is slight: ritual is simply *doing* the symbol. If a hug is a symbol, hugging is the ritual; shared food may be a symbol, sharing it is the ritual; flowers can be a symbol, putting them on a grave is a ritual. Like symbols, rituals cannot be "explained." Who could put into words all we "mean" when we hug a crying child? Who would even attempt to explain what you "mean" when you put flowers on your mother's grave?

HOW SYMBOLS WORK

A symbol works by pointing beyond itself. It *signifies meaning beyond what meets the eye.* But—AND THIS IS CRUCIALLY IM-PORTANT—*a symbol works precisely by being itself.* If the hug is perfunctory, if the flowers artificial . . . the symbol doesn't work. In the Christian eucharist, for example, the essential symbol is bread broken and shared, wine poured out and shared. If the wine *isn't* shared, and if the bread is too small to be broken or shared, or participants are served leftovers from last week, the power of that symbol is lost. A symbol only points *beyond* itself when it is true *to itself.*

That a symbol works by pointing beyond itself is clear even from the meaning of the Greek word: *sym-bol* means "to put together." A symbol puts together the thing-in-itself and what it points to beyond itself. It also puts us together. (The opposite of *sym-bol,* by the way, is *dia-bol:* to divide, to separate. Telling someone that "an egg is the symbol for the resurrection" is literally diabolic! Handing someone an egg on Easter morning, with a smile and the words "Christ is risen!"—that's *sym-bolic.*)

WHAT SYMBOLS DO FOR US

Symbols and rituals put us together; they express meaning for us; they identify us. They let me know who I am, what is important to me, where I belong, where I am at home. They heal. They make me whole.

Ritual isn't something we do out of obligation, but from neces-sity. It's a need—a *gnawing* human need—as essential to our lives as food. Our everyday lives demand that we have occasions to stop being partial and to be put back together, to be healed and made whole. Ritual is unique among human activities in that it is always concerned with wholeness, with the totality of our lives, with ultimates. We simply can't live—humanly—without it.

THREE NOTES

(1) Since we can't live without it, it is important that we un-derstand it. The essence of ritual is *play:* doing apparently useless things with great solemnity, fantasizing in our hearts the ultimate realities, engaging in that excess which is always a part of festivity

and celebration. Unfortunately, our pragmatic and rationalistic culture discourages us from play, from fantasy, from paying attention to things-in-themselves, so essential to symbol, ritual, and celebration.

Despite our culture, the fact remains that we *are* powerfully influenced by what we see and hear, touch, feel, smell, and taste, as well as by what we sense in unconscious, intuitive, "extra" sensory ways. That's why ritual has to be *multi*-sensory, and why we have to use the traditional symbols and rituals broadly and fully, letting them speak for themselves in their own profound way.

(2) Perhaps the greatest error made in regard to symbol and ritual—an error made by priests and parents alike, as well as by professional religious educators—is to identify ritual with words, or to feel that symbols won't work unless they are accompanied by numerous words of explanation. In religious ritual, especially, we must be aware of the *limits* of words, of instruction and verbalization *about* symbols. The emphasis has to be on the nonverbal—on the intuitive and on body language. (The body proclaims as much as the voice; the very way we stand, walk, and handle things speaks loudly.) We must let the symbols speak for themselves. Words can be part of a ritual, of course; but we must strive for great simplicity of verbal expression. If we *do* use words, they must really count.

(3) In religious ritual we strive to be at the height of our God-consciousness and therefore at the height of our human consciousness. Whether at the altar of a church or at our supper table, the primary attitude in ritual is reverence: a sense of the holy, the sacred, of the *numinous* behind things; a sense of mystery which we ourselves are. In ritual, this feeling of the "beyond" is indispensable. It is this awareness which makes celebration possible; it is, indeed, what celebration is all about. There *is* more to us than meets the eye: we are the dwelling place of the Most High.

CELEBRATION

Whether our celebration is an Easter sunrise service, a birthday party for a two-year-old, or something as simple as a glass of wine with Friday night supper, three things are always involved: (1) a special occasion, when we (2) step out of our ordinary everyday business-as-usual world, with (3) a heightened awareness of that greater reality which gives wider perspective to and supports our everyday lives.

Everyone nowadays knows what "consciousness raising" means, thanks to the women's movement. Probably the best definition of celebration would be *"conscious* consciousness raising": the raising up, in heightened awareness, of ourselves and the world in thanksgiving and praise.

But we can celebrate only if we are convinced in our hearts that "at bottom everything that is, is good, and that it is *good* to exist." We can choose the occasion for a celebration (anniversaries of births, deaths, wedding; the changing of the seasons, new moons and solstices, etc.), and we can determine *how* we celebrate (which always involves beautiful things to delight in, tasty foods, music, etc.), but we cannot determine *what. What* we celebrate is gift, "grace." We celebrate what has been given to us: the goodness of the world, our delight in being created, our sharing in the life of God, the overcoming of death. If our lives include the experience of such "grace," then we cannot *not* celebrate.

Well . . . may these brief comments serve, if nothing else, as the autumn leaves falling through these pages, as an eventual compost to nurture your own reflections on these important topics. (Sam Mackintosh, from *Greenblade*, November, 1980. *Greenblade* began as a homespun mimeographed newsletter. In August, 1981, it appeared under the title *Family Festivals* for the first time. *Family Festivals* is published by Resource Publications, Box 444, Saratoga, CA 95070. Sam continues as editor.)

Appendix D

Guidelines for Relationship of Accountability*

1. What is the minimum daily time to which you commit yourself for quiet, prayer, reading Scripture, and journaling? At least one-half hour is recommended if you are just taking on this discipline. Keep a close account of the time you are spending and record it in your journal.

2. Do you prefer to select your own Scripture or have one assigned to you? Work with only one chapter a week. Let it speak to you where you are. Become involved with it. Write about it.

3. Record your thoughts and feelings in a journal at some point in your meditation.

4. Include the following in your written report:
   a. Were you faithful each day? Which areas did you miss? Which were the most difficult for you? Be specific in reporting time.
   b. What were the highs and lows of your week? Where did you celebrate? Where grieve?
   c. Where did God speak to you through his written Word?
   d. What time and where did you step outside yourself and become engaged in the world's suffering at some point?

5. What is your practice in the area of stewardship and weekly worship with your community?

6. Are there further disciplines for which you wish to be held accountable? (Dieting, fasting, physical fitness, time spent with family, etc.)

7. Use an 8½" x 11" sheet of paper for your written report. Write down the left-hand side, leaving the other half open for comments.

*The material in this Appendix is from the Wellspring Mission Group, The Church of the Saviour, Washington, D.C.